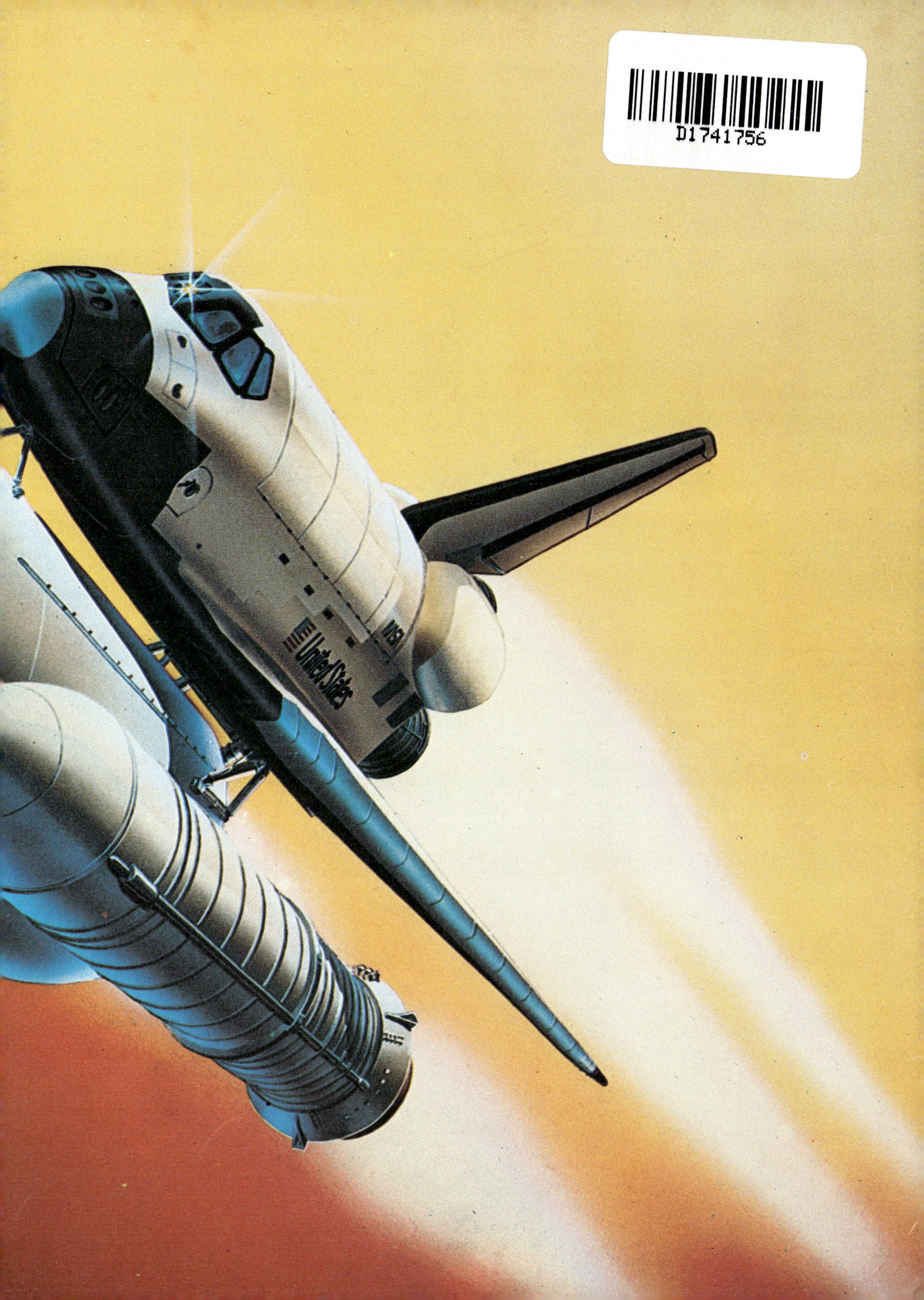

For dear Huntly
Christmas 1982
From Mum & Dad,

THE STORY OF THE SPACE SHUTTLE

THE STORY OF
THE SPACE SHUTTLE

Tim Furniss

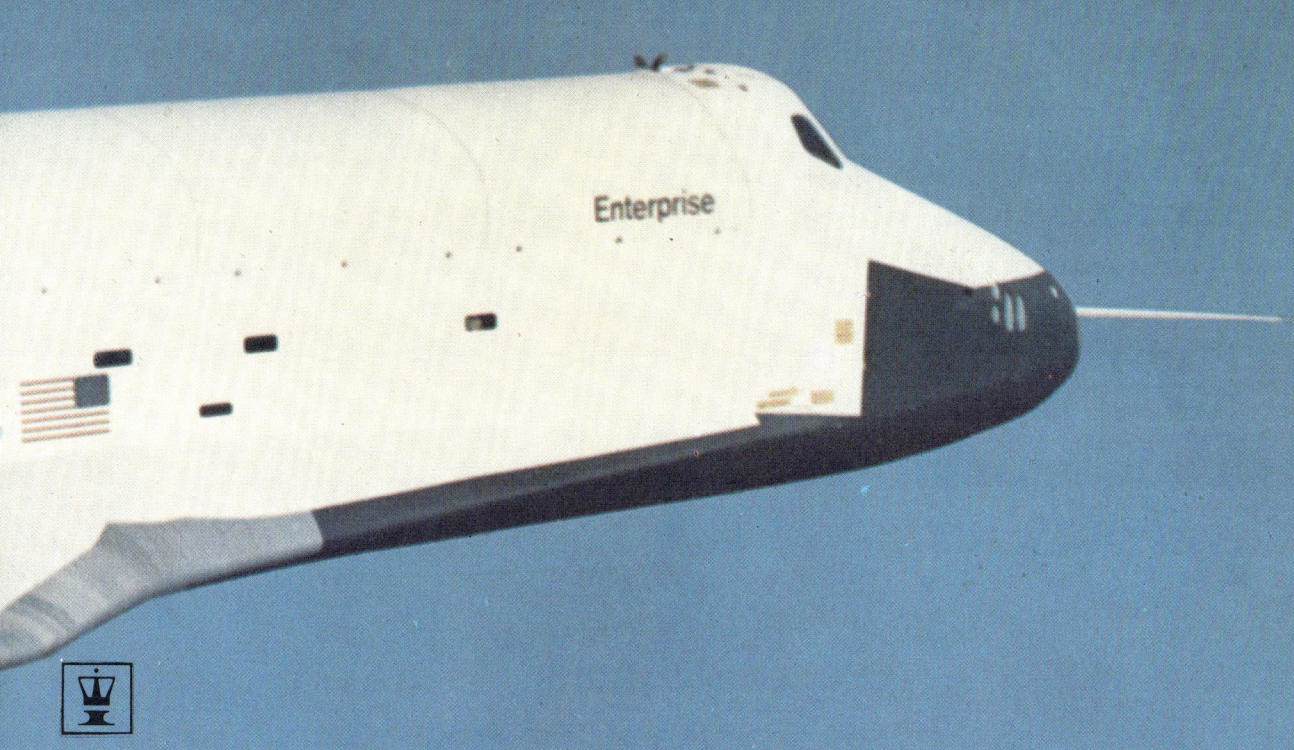

Enterprise

HODDER AND STOUGHTON
LONDON SYDNEY AUCKLAND TORONTO

Printed in Great Britain for Hodder & Stoughton Children's Books, a
division of Hodder and Stoughton Ltd, Mill Road, Dunton Green, Sevenoaks,
Kent TN13 2YJ (Editorial Office: 47 Bedford Square, London WC1B 3DP), by
Morrison & Gibb Ltd, London & Edinburgh.
Photoset by Rowland Phototypesetting Ltd, Bury St. Edmunds, Suffolk.

CONTENTS

To Sue with love

BIRTH OF THE SPACE SHUTTLE   1

Since the Space Age began, with the launching of Sputnik 1 on
4 October 1957, thousands of satellites and space probes have been
sent both into orbit and to the Moon and planets.

While the spacecraft themselves perform useful tasks and make
interesting discoveries, to get them into space costs a great deal of
money and has led to wastage. Rocket stages used to propel these
craft fall back to Earth, break up and sink in the sea; some are lost
during re-entry into the Earth's atmosphere, some are still in orbit
and some have even crashed on to the Moon.

Space is littered with garbage. Not only is there wastage in
terms of spent rocket stages, but also in the form of dead satellites
which still orbit the Earth, their jobs complete: useless chunks of metal
waiting for re-entry into the atmosphere or doomed to infinite flight
in perpetual orbit.

Nothing that is launched is used again. Even spacecraft that
return to Earth and are recovered, like those containing astronauts,
are not reused. They end up in museums after their one and only
flight.

As far as is known, only one spacecraft has ever flown twice. That
was Gemini 2 which flew into space in 1965 and again in 1966
during a flight test for the Manned Orbital Laboratory programme.

On 16 July 1969, a 365-foot high rocket with a spacecraft at the
top of it was launched from Pad 39 at Cape Canaveral. The rocket was
called Saturn 5. The spacecraft was called Apollo 11 and inside it
were three men, two of whom were destined to be the first ever to
land on the Moon.

It cost £140 million to fly the Apollo 11 mission. The majority of
the rocket and spacecraft combination was discarded and what did
return never flew again. The first stage, which developed a mammoth 7.5 million pounds of thrust, fell away and crashed into the
sea. The second stage, its job complete, was ejected and broke up,
littering the Atlantic Ocean with yet more metallic garbage. Stage

Right – the first manned lunar landing mission Apollo 11 takes off on a Saturn 5 rocket, 16 July 1969. The mission cost £140 million, and no part of the equipment was reusable.

Below – Britain from space. Information gained from photographs like this is valuable to many sciences and will be more easily and cheaply obtained when the Space Shuttle is in operation.

three fired long enough to place Apollo 11 into an Earth parking orbit and then fired again to send the three men on a trajectory towards the Moon. The spent rocket stage then separated from Apollo and flew on, passed the Moon and became an artificial planet of the Sun.

Apollo's Command, Service and Lunar Modules, free of 330 feet of rocket, flew on to the Moon and entered orbit around it. The Lunar Module descended to the surface taking Neil Armstrong and Buzz Aldrin into the history books. Later, the astronauts placed equipment on the surface. They took off into lunar orbit using the descent stage of the Lunar Module as a launch pad which was left on the surface of the Moon.

The ascent stage docked with the Command and Service Module, and, after the astronauts had transferred themselves and their moon rocks into the Command Module, it was discarded and left orbiting the Moon. Now only the Command and Service module combination was left. The Service Module's engine fired and took Armstrong, Aldrin and their companion, Mike Collins, out of lunar orbit on a course for home. Three days later, as the spacemen hurtled towards the Earth at 25,000 mph, the Service Module was discarded and destroyed in the Earth's atmosphere during a fiery re-entry which the Command Module, protected by a heatshield, survived.

This 12-foot high Command Module splashed down in the Pacific Ocean beneath three red and white striped parachutes: all that was left of the 365-feet-high vehicle that was dispatched from the launch pad. It had cost about £500 to launch every pound of Apollo 11. All that returned was a small spacecraft which could not be used again, three safe, heroic and famous astronauts and some moon rocks.

It was at about this time that scientists were putting serious thought into the development of something that had often been written about in science fiction stories – the reusable spacecraft that could shuttle backwards and forwards from space many times.

So the Space Shuttle was conceived. Its task: to reduce the cost of space travel, making the exploration and use of space a more cost-effective and viable proposition.

The immediate problems to solve were how to launch a rocket, recover it and use it again and how to build a spacecraft that could survive re-entry into the Earth's atmosphere to such an extent that it could be reused.

Firstly, scientists looked at the possibilities of building a rocket-spacecraft, a one-piece vehicle that could be launched, fly in space and land. This proved too difficult and was not cost-effective because of the absolutely enormous expense that would be required to build and develop such a vehicle.

Next, the two-piece space shuttle was designed – two gliders fixed together: one, a rocket booster that would carry the shuttle glider into space piggy-back style, then fall away to make a piloted landing; and, two, the manned space orbiting craft that would later return to Earth like an aircraft.

Another scheme envisaged the use of a reusable space glider which could be launched piggy-back style on the back of an existing rocket which could parachute to Earth to be used again. One such rocket considered was a modification of Saturn 5 which was used to launch Apollo.

Problems were encountered in many areas, the main one being cost. Could these vehicles be developed within the limited budget

Early versions of the Space Shuttle: on the left, the reusable shuttle on top of the Saturn 5 first stage; on the right, a reusable fly-back piloted rocket booster with the Shuttle space-plane riding piggy-back style on its back.

available? After all, the scientists did not have an open brief to spend as much as it took to develop a shuttle vehicle. What had to be considered were development and operational costs plus suitability. In other words, the overall economics of the system – launch costs against building costs.

It was at about this time that the President of the United States, Richard Nixon, gave the go-ahead to produce a reusable space shuttle. The time had come to stop theorising and to start designing and building the vehicle. The Space Shuttle was born on 5 January 1972, when Nixon made this statement to the world:

'I have decided today that the United States should proceed at once with the development of an entirely new type of space transportation system designed to help transform the space frontier of the 1970s into familiar territory, easily accessible for human endeavour in the 1980s and '90s.

'This system will centre on a space vehicle that can shuttle repeatedly from Earth to orbit and back. It will revolutionise transportation into near space, by routinising it. It will take the astronomical costs out of astronautics. In short, it will go a long way toward delivering the rich benefits of practical space utilisation and the valuable spin-offs from space efforts into the daily lives of Americans and all people.

'However, all these possibilities, and countless others with direct and dramatic bearing on human betterment, can never be more than fractionally realised so long as every single trip from Earth to orbit remains a matter of special effort and staggering expense. This is why commitment to the Space Shuttle programme is the right next step for America to take, in moving out from our present beach-head in the sky to achieve a real working presence in space – because the Space Shuttle will give us routine access to space by sharply reducing costs in dollars and preparation time.'

Intensive engineering studies were conducted by the American space agency, NASA (National Aeronautics and Space Administration) and aerospace companies in order to find the final, most cost-effective design of the Shuttle. While the rocket glider/space glider combination would be the cheapest to operate, its development costs would far outweigh this advantage. A reusable Shuttle launched by more conventional rocket boosters would be slightly more expensive to operate in the long term but cheaper to develop in the short term. This was the avenue followed by NASA.

So, the studies really concentrated on what type of rocket booster to use and how to make it reusable. On 15 March 1972, it was announced that the Shuttle would be launched by two solid propellant rocket stages. At launch, the Shuttle's own engines would also be firing, but its fuel tank would not be part of the Shuttle but a separate structure on which the Shuttle would be mounted. This was called an external tank and would be the only expendable part of the system. The solid rocket stages would parachute into the ocean and be recovered.

The decision to build this version of the Shuttle was made because information showed that the solid rocket system offered lower development costs and lower technical risk. And it would be easier to develop with less chance of technical teething problems. Studies also showed that this method would provide the highest rate of return on investment. It would now cost only £50 to launch one pound of payload into space instead of £500 as in the case of Apollo.

By this time, when Man had learned to conquer space and was discovering how to use it effectively, developing the Shuttle seemed a natural thing to do.

After all, do we throw an airliner away when it lands at London Airport after a transatlantic flight from New York?

The Space Shuttle, consisting of an Orbiter vehicle riding on top of an external tank containing fuel, to which are attached two solid rocket boosters. Only the external tank cannot be used again.

2 THE SPACE SHUTTLE SYSTEM

The Space Shuttle is called the Space Transportation System, or STS as it is abbreviated in space jargon. It is a combination of vehicles: part rocket, part spacecraft and part aircraft. The Shuttle is a very strange, awkward-looking object when poised for action on the launch pad, protruding into the sky like a moth resting on the stem of a flower. It's hard to believe that this combination of craft can fly, let alone reach orbit. Yet the Space Transportation System is the most sophisticated and advanced space machine ever built. It will radically alter and even revolutionise the future use and exploration of space.

The Space Shuttle consists of an Orbiter vehicle, a large liquid fuel tank and two solid fuel rocket boosters. The rocket boosters are stacked vertically, either side of the fuel tank on which the Orbiter is positioned. The Orbiter is the main component, the part of the system which flies in space, the vehicle that carries a crew and passengers.

The solid rocket boosters, or SRBs as they are called, provide power during launch together with engines on the Orbiter. They are called solid rocket boosters because they are propelled by the burning of solid fuel, rather like sophisticated gunpowder. Most rockets are powered by the burning of liquid fuels called propellants, such as liquid oxygen, liquid hydrogen and kerosene. The Space Shuttle is actually powered by both liquid and solid fuels. The Orbiter's own engines operate using liquid oxygen and liquid hydrogen and it is these liquids that are stored in the external tank, called the ET, to which the Orbiter and the solid rocket boosters are attached.

So, at launch, the Space Shuttle is firing on five engines, two using solid fuel and three using liquid fuel. At lift-off these engines generate a thrust of over six million pounds. This makes the Shuttle the most powerful rocket combination since the mammoth Saturn 5 rocket which sent men to the Moon beneath engines giving out a thrust of over seven million pounds. The launch of the Shuttle is

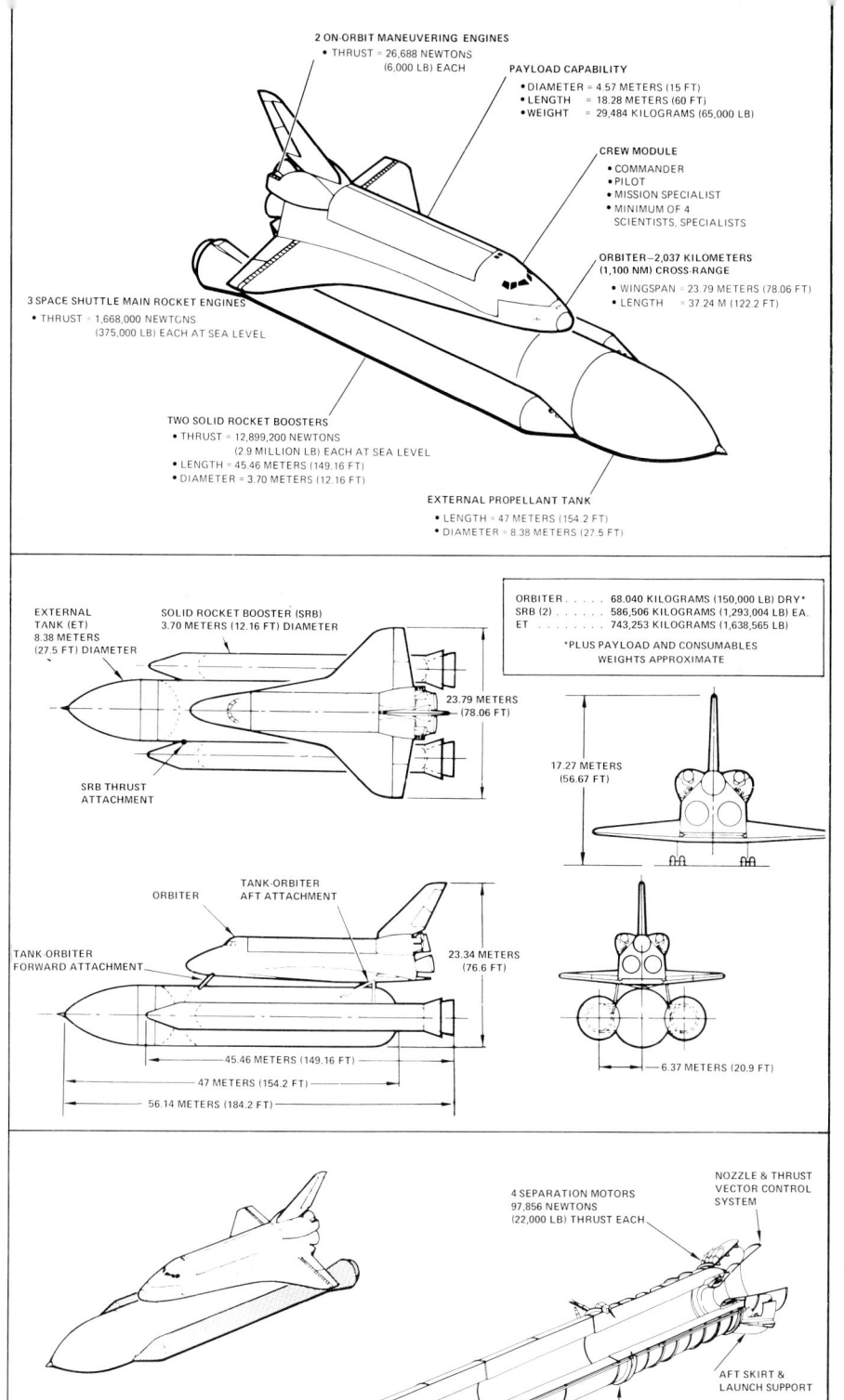

2 ON-ORBIT MANEUVERING ENGINES
- THRUST = 26,688 NEWTONS (6,000 LB) EACH

PAYLOAD CAPABILITY
- DIAMETER = 4.57 METERS (15 FT)
- LENGTH = 18.28 METERS (60 FT)
- WEIGHT = 29,484 KILOGRAMS (65,000 LB)

CREW MODULE
- COMMANDER
- PILOT
- MISSION SPECIALIST
- MINIMUM OF 4 SCIENTISTS, SPECIALISTS

ORBITER—2,037 KILOMETERS (1,100 NM) CROSS-RANGE
- WINGSPAN = 23.79 METERS (78.06 FT)
- LENGTH = 37.24 M (122.2 FT)

3 SPACE SHUTTLE MAIN ROCKET ENGINES
- THRUST = 1,668,000 NEWTONS (375,000 LB) EACH AT SEA LEVEL

TWO SOLID ROCKET BOOSTERS
- THRUST = 12,899,200 NEWTONS (2.9 MILLION LB) EACH AT SEA LEVEL
- LENGTH = 45.46 METERS (149.16 FT)
- DIAMETER = 3.70 METERS (12.16 FT)

EXTERNAL PROPELLANT TANK
- LENGTH = 47 METERS (154.2 FT)
- DIAMETER = 8.38 METERS (27.5 FT)

The Space Shuttle Transportation System

EXTERNAL TANK (ET) 8.38 METERS (27.5 FT) DIAMETER

SOLID ROCKET BOOSTER (SRB) 3.70 METERS (12.16 FT) DIAMETER

ORBITER . . . . . 68,040 KILOGRAMS (150,000 LB) DRY*
SRB (2) . . . . . 586,506 KILOGRAMS (1,293,004 LB) EA.
ET . . . . . 743,253 KILOGRAMS (1,638,565 LB)
*PLUS PAYLOAD AND CONSUMABLES WEIGHTS APPROXIMATE

23.79 METERS (78.06 FT)

SRB THRUST ATTACHMENT

17.27 METERS (56.67 FT)

ORBITER

TANK-ORBITER AFT ATTACHMENT

TANK-ORBITER FORWARD ATTACHMENT

23.34 METERS (76.6 FT)

45.46 METERS (149.16 FT)

47 METERS (154.2 FT)

56.14 METERS (184.2 FT)

6.37 METERS (20.9 FT)

Dimensions

4 SEPARATION MOTORS 97,856 NEWTONS (22,000 LB) THRUST EACH

NOZZLE & THRUST VECTOR CONTROL SYSTEM

AFT SKIRT & LAUNCH SUPPORT

SOLID ROCKET BOOSTER/EXTERNAL TANK ATTACH RING, AFT AVIONICS AND SWAY BRACES

MAIN CHUTE PACK

4 SEPARATION MOTORS 96,432 NEWTONS (21,680 LB) THRUST EACH

SOLID ROCKET BOOSTER/ EXTERNAL TANK THRUST ATTACH

DROGUE CHUTE

NOSE FAIRING

FORWARD SKIRT

SEPARATION AVIONICS, OPERATIONAL FLIGHT INSTRUMENTATION, RECOVERY AVIONICS, AND RANGE SAFETY SYSTEM

The solid rocket booster

DIMENSIONS (EACH)	
LENGTH	45.46 METERS (149.16 FT)
DIAMETER	3.70 METERS (12.16 FT)
GROSS WEIGHT	586,506 KILOGRAMS (1,293,004 LB)
INERT WEIGHT	82,879 KILOGRAMS (182,714 LB)
PROPELLANT WEIGHT	503,627 KILOGRAMS (1,110,290 LB)
THRUST (SEA LEVEL)	12,899,200 NEWTONS SEA LEVEL (2,900,000 LB)
WEIGHTS APPROXIMATE	

faster than that of a liquid-fuelled rocket such as the Saturn 5, which rose slowly and ponderously from the launch pad. The Shuttle zooms skyward beneath almost solid-looking tongues of flame and smoke.

The Orbiter, which rides piggyback-style on the back of the external tank, to which are attached the solid rocket boosters, is the key to the Space Transportation System. It is designed to travel in orbit for missions lasting seven to 30 days, returning to Earth through a fiery re-entry and landing like an aircraft. It is to be used over and over again – up to 100 times before a major overhaul and service is necessary.

The first space aeroplane, the Orbiter has stubby delta wings which have a span of 78 feet. It is 122 feet long, which makes it about as large as a DC-9 airliner. In its fuselage is a cargo bay with two doors which can be opened in space, exposing a payload, equipment that is carried on into space by a rocket. Such a payload is the Spacelab space station. This cargo bay is called the payload bay and it can hold cargo up to 15 feet wide and 60 feet long. The heaviest payload that can be carried is 65,000 pounds, equivalent to over 30,000 bags of sugar. Some of this weight is shed in space because the Shuttle can only make a safe landing with a cargo of 32,000 pounds in the payload bay. This is not a problem, since one of the jobs of the Shuttle is to deploy satellites and space probes in orbit, thus reducing the weight in the cargo hold.

To lift satellites out of the payload bay and place them in orbit and to collect satellites in need of repair, the Shuttle is equipped with a manipulator arm. This allows the crew to handle the payloads by remote control with the aid of a TV camera. The astronauts use a TV monitor in the cockpit.

The cockpit is at the nose of the Shuttle Orbiter. This is on the upper deck of the spacecraft. It holds four astronauts – a commander, a pilot and two mission specialists. Beneath them on the lower deck will be seats for up to three passengers, payload specialists who are being sent into space to operate their own equipment and experiments. Also in the lower deck are the living quarters for seven men and women and the control equipment for experiments and instruments which are in the payload bay. The living quarters include toilets, a kitchen and a shower room, as well as sleeping berths.

For early test flights, in which only two astronauts are flying, the Orbiter is equipped with ejection seats. These are similar to those fitted to the Gemini two-man spacecraft which were launched between 1965 and 1966. On later operational flights no ejection systems will be used because it would not be practical to fit them for all crewmen. Also by this time it is hoped that the Shuttle will have been proved such a reliable system that the possible need for ejection due to launch failure will have been reduced.

The key to the success of the Space Shuttle system is the ability of the Orbiter to withstand the fiery heat of re-entry and still be able to fly again for up to 100 missions.

During re-entry, a satellite that has been in orbit is travelling so quickly that, when it hits the upper layer of the Earth's atmosphere, friction against it causes it to heat up. If it is not protected by a heatshield it burns up. On all the earlier manned spaceflights, the spacecraft's heatshield was ablative. This means that the major part of the heatshield literally burned away during re-entry, thus absorbing the heat and protecting the spacecraft and its occupants. But after one flight, the spacecraft could not be used again unless it was completely rebuilt and given a new heatshield. So the Shuttle had to be fitted with a new type of non-ablative heatshield, one which could absorb the heat but still protect the spacecraft. The new development was the ceramic fibre tile. These tiles heat up rather like the grills of a gas fire at home. Then, having survived the heat

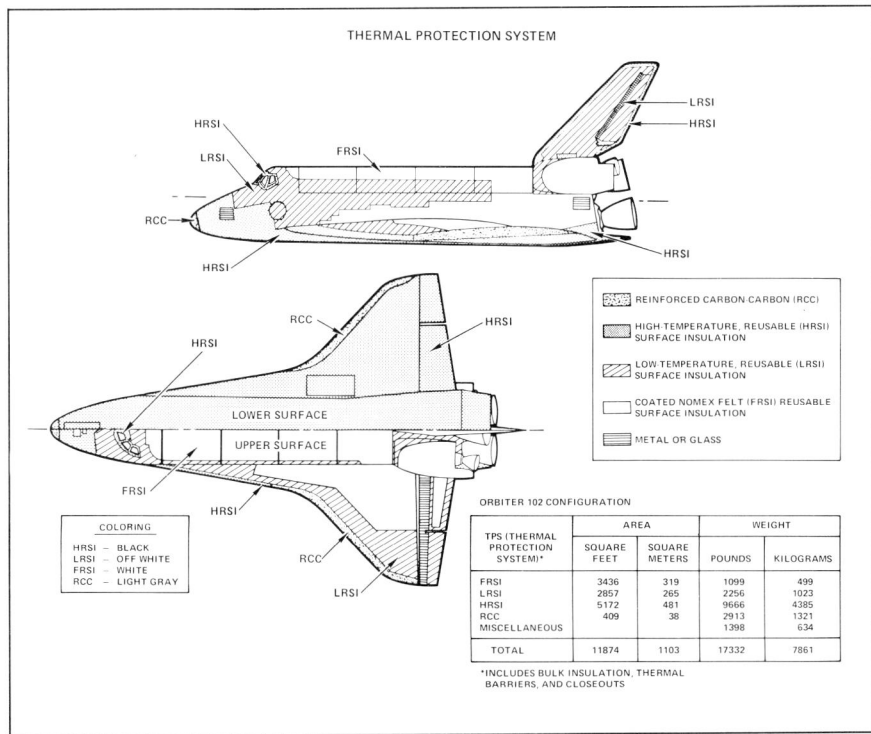

Thermal protection system – the key to the Space Shuttle system. 34,250 tiles of different materials enable the Orbiter to withstand the fiery heat of re-entry to the Earth's atmosphere.

generated by the fiery re-entry, they cool down again.

The Orbiter heatshield is called a passive thermal protection system, or TPS for short. It consists of different strengths of material because, as the Orbiter re-enters, some parts of the craft become much hotter than others. Re-entry is made at an angle, rather like that of an airliner coming in to land at an airport, with the underside of the craft taking all the friction against the air-stream. The hottest parts of the Orbiter, therefore, are the leading edges of the wings and the nose, which glow red during re-entry. They heat up to 1600°C. These areas are fitted with 'bricks' or 'tiles' comprising a material called carbon-carbon. This consists of carbon fibres with a resin coating of a chemical called silicon carbide. Most of the underside and sides of the Orbiter heat up to about 1260°C and these areas are fitted with fibre tiles. Other parts of the Orbiter such as its top are heated to about 398°C and these are equipped with a felt fibre material. A total of 34,250 tiles of these various materials covers the Orbiter. They represent one of the greatest advances in space technology, for without them there would be no reusable Space Shuttle system.

Electrical power for the Space Shuttle and its payloads is generated by three fuel cells that use liquid hydrogen and liquid oxygen. The fuel cells are in the forward end of the Orbiter mid-fuselage. During peak and average power conditions, only two fuel cells are used. The quantities of fuel (hydrogen and oxygen) normally carried by the Orbiter will be enough to generate about 1,530 kilowatt hours of energy. The amount includes 50 kilowatt hours of energy required by a typical payload for a seven-day mission. If additional power is needed, separate fuel kits may be carried aboard, each kit supplying enough fuel for an additional 840 kilowatt hours of energy.

A by-product of the chemical conversion of hydrogen and oxygen to obtain electrical energy is the production of water. All the water for human consumption aboard the Shuttle is supplied from the by-products of the fuel cells.

The Orbiter's communication antennae, about 20 of them, are flush mounted on the forward fuselage. Throughout the mission the Orbiter will provide direct voice, signal and television communications with the ground crew, crewmen on space walks and with detached payloads through its communications system and a network of ground stations and communications satellites.

Another essential part of the Space Shuttle Orbiter is its main engine system. This is called the SSME. The Orbiter is equipped

One of the main engines
under test at Bay St
Louis.

with three of these engines, each with a thrust of 470,000 pounds.
They burn liquid oxygen and liquid hydrogen, which are fed to the
combustion chambers of the engines, where they light up or are
ignited, from the external tank on which the Orbiter is positioned at
lift-off and during the ascent into space. These engines are the most
efficient yet designed and represent another new development in
space technology. Basically, the engines pre-burn the propellants
before their entry into the final combustion areas in the thrust
chamber and this makes the generation of thrust more efficient by
raising the temperature and pressure of the propellants.

Each engine is controlled by an on-board computer system, an electronic digital control, nicknamed not surprisingly the 'controller'. This system accepts and processes vehicle signals and issues start and shutdown commands, regulating the thrust of the rockets and monitoring general engine operation, taking automatic corrective measures if necessary. These engines are throttleable between 60% and 109% of their maximum design thrust, rather like an accelerator and overdrive on a car.

The three engines fire simultaneously for eight minutes during the launching, consuming 1122 pounds of fuel per second. Just a few seconds before orbital speed, 17,500 mph, has been achieved the engines shut down. The external tank is discarded and the Orbiter's two smaller engines take over for the final seconds. These engines are called the orbital manoeuvring system or OMS.

Each OMS engine has a thrust of 6000 pounds. They are powered by chemicals called nitrogen tetroxide and momomethyl hydrazine and are designed to operate for all 100 scheduled missions, during which time they will have been fired about 1000 times for a total period of around 15 hours. These engines are designed not only to achieve the necessary speed to allow the spacecraft to reach orbit, but also to change the altitude by altering the speed of the Orbiter around the Earth. They are also used to fire the spacecraft into the atmosphere for re-entry.

The Orbiter is able to carry additional OMS packs for greater manoeuvrability.

To allow the spacecraft to perform manoeuvres in space like turning over and around, turning from one side to another and positioning itself pointing either upwards or downwards, the Orbiter has a reaction control system. This consists of 38 thrusters which, when fired in short bursts, can allow the Orbiter to perform these movements, which are called roll, yaw and pitch respectively.

Thirty-two of these motors have a thrust of 900 pounds and six of them impart a thrust of 25 pounds. Fourteen are situated on the Orbiter's nose and 24 in the tail, twelve in the area of each OMS engine. These are also fuelled by nitrogen tetroxide and momomethyl hydrazine.

After its fuel has been depleted, just a few seconds before orbit has been achieved, the external tank is ejected. It is the only part of the Space Shuttle system that is not reusable. It burns up in the atmosphere. The external tank is the largest part of the Space Shuttle system and is the largest liquid oxygen, liquid hydrogen structure ever built. Its internal volume is six times that of the American space station, Skylab, which was launched in 1973.

The tank is 153 feet long, almost as tall as Nelson's Column, and

It is 27 feet wide. It holds 226,000 pounds of liquid hydrogen and 1,324,000 pounds of liquid oxygen.

Attached to the external tank and providing the initial extra launching thrust for the first 124 seconds of the flight of the Shuttle are the solid rocket boosters, or SRBs. These take the rocket-space-plane combination to a height of 28 miles. Each booster is 12 feet in diameter and 149 feet high. They each carry 1,100,000 pounds of solid fuel and generate a thrust of 2,650,000 pounds. The thrust is reduced by one third as the Shuttle goes through a period of maximum dynamic pressure, the period during which the greatest stress is placed on the accelerating vehicle. This takes place at 55 seconds after lift-off, called T + 55 seconds. At burnout, when the rockets stop firing, at T + 124 seconds, each booster is ejected. They

Left – the external tank.

Below – one of the solid rocket boosters being assembled.

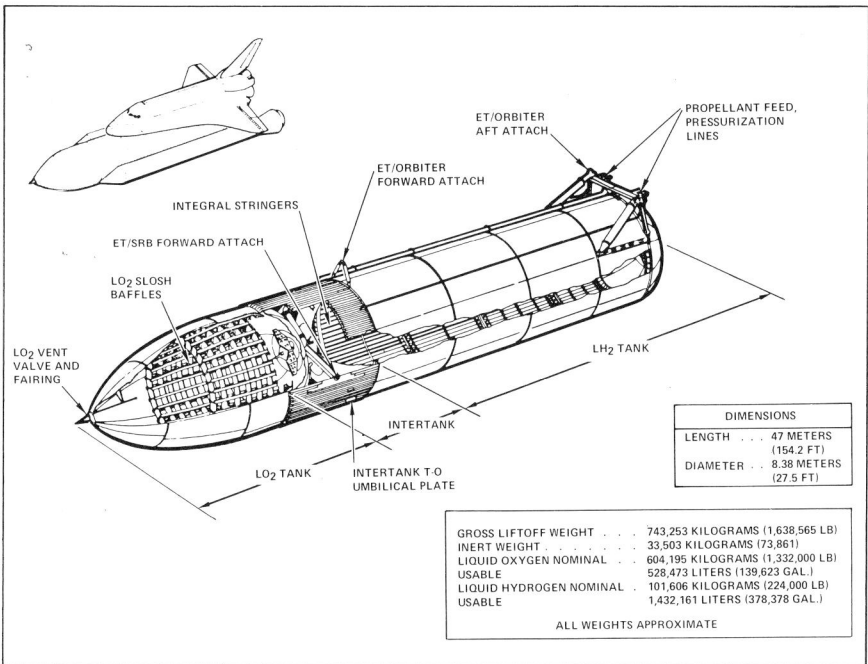

ET/ORBITER AFT ATTACH

PROPELLANT FEED, PRESSURIZATION LINES

ET/ORBITER FORWARD ATTACH

INTEGRAL STRINGERS

ET/SRB FORWARD ATTACH

LO₂ SLOSH BAFFLES

LO₂ VENT VALVE AND FAIRING

LH₂ TANK

INTERTANK

LO₂ TANK

INTERTANK T-O UMBILICAL PLATE

DIMENSIONS	
LENGTH . . .	47 METERS (154.2 FT)
DIAMETER . .	8.38 METERS (27.5 FT)

GROSS LIFTOFF WEIGHT . . .	743,253 KILOGRAMS (1,638,565 LB)
INERT WEIGHT	33,503 KILOGRAMS (73,861)
LIQUID OXYGEN NOMINAL . .	604,195 KILOGRAMS (1,332,000 LB)
USABLE	528,473 LITERS (139,623 GAL.)
LIQUID HYDROGEN NOMINAL .	101,606 KILOGRAMS (224,000 LB)
USABLE	1,432,161 LITERS (378,378 GAL.)

ALL WEIGHTS APPROXIMATE

The boosters are jettisoned. They will parachute down into the ocean, to be recovered and used again.

coast to a height of 41 miles on a ballistic 'up-and-down' trajectory and fall back to Earth. A parachute opens and each booster descends into the ocean. The boosters are retrieved and towed to land for refurbishment and reuse on later flights. They are designed to be flown at least twenty times. To increase the Shuttle's boosting power and lifting capability, the thrust of the solid rocket boosters will later be augmented by the addition of small 'strap on' solid rockets to the SRBs themselves.

That's the System. How it flies is described in Chapter 7.

SPACELAB

In 1981, during one of the later operational missions of the Space Shuttle, Orbiter No. 102 will begin circling the Earth. Soon afterwards its payload bay doors will slowly open, exposing to space a cylindrical structure with a tunnel connecting it to the Shuttle cockpit. This will be Spacelab 1 and travelling and working inside it will be the first Western European astronaut.

What is interesting about Spacelab is that it is European. An extremely important part of the Space Shuttle programme, the European Spacelab will provide a facility for scientific work for both European and American scientists. The first Spacelab will carry a European with the crew and the second Spacelab will be an all-American mission. Over 100 Spacelab missions will follow.

Spacelab was born in 1973, when the nine member countries of the newly-formed European Space Agency (ESA) and the United States signed an agreement concerning 'the development, procurement and use of a space laboratory in conjunction with the Space Shuttle system'.

The nine member countries of ESA are Belgium, Denmark, the Federal Republic of Germany, France, Italy, the Netherlands, Spain, Switzerland and the United Kingdom. In addition, Austria, an ESA non-member, will be contributing to the programme. Aerospace companies in these countries are building the components of the Spacelab under the supervision of ESA and NASA, the American space agency.

ESA's part of the agreement with the United States is that they will develop, manufacture, test and deliver to NASA the Spacelab flight unit, an engineering test module, spare parts, two sets of ground support equipment, engineering support, plus additional Spacelabs when the time comes. Spacelab is costing about £300 million, and this cost is being borne by the ESA countries.

Spacelab is a very versatile space station because it is developed on what is called a modular basis, and for each mission comprises separate pieces which can be put together in different configurations depending on the tasks that are to be performed.

It has two principal components. The first of these is the pressurised module. This is the laboratory with a 'shirt-sleeve' environment. The second component is the open pallet which exposes materials and equipment directly to space.

Each pressurised module consists of different parts, or segments, to permit additional flight flexibility. One is called the core segment. This contains supporting sub-systems, such as data processing computer equipment and services for both pressurised modules and experiment pallets. It also has laboratory fixtures such as floor mounted racks and work benches, supplies and appropriate working space.

The second segment is the experiment segment or module. This provides more laboratory working space. The configuration of this segment depends on the mission being flown and if it is not necessary this segment is not included.

Each of these pressurised segments, the core and experiment segments, is a cylinder 13½ feet in diameter and nine feet long. When two segments are assembled together with end cones their maximum outside length is 23 feet.

A tunnel connects the pressurised laboratory with the pressurised cabin of the Orbiter. The tunnel also consists of segments. Its length and the way it is made up therefore varies depending on the length and the number and type of Spacelab segments. An airlock module can be attached to the tunnel to permit scientist-astronauts to get out of the spacecraft and walk in space, perhaps to retrieve science packages on the outside of the space station in a pallet at the end of Spacelab.

There are five pallet segments available on each Spacelab mission. Each is 10 feet long. They not only provide a platform for mounting instruments but can also be used to cool equipment taken out of the lab by an astronaut during a space walk, or EVA.

Some flights may just fly with these pallets and no pressurised segments, in which case the structure will have a total length of 49 feet. These pallets contain experiments which are kept in an equipment housing called an igloo.

The pallets are designed for large instruments, experiments requiring direct exposure to the space environment or those needing unobstructed or broad fields of view. Such equipment includes telescopes, antennae and sensors such as radiometers.

Spacelab can not only be modified for a variety of missions but will also be reusable. Each Spacelab module is designed to last five years or fifty space missions, whichever is completed first. Specifically, Spacelab is intended to 'provide versatile space laboratory and observatory facilities at low initial costs and low operating costs; reduce preparatory time for space experimentation, and provide for international participation in space'.

The planned length of each Spacelab mission is seven days, although missions up to 30 days may be performed.

The total weight of each Spacelab cannot exceed the landing capability of the Orbiter which holds it. This is 32,000 pounds. A Spacelab comprising only of modules will weigh 12,195 pounds, comprising only of pallets, 20,062 pounds, and a module plus a pallet, 12,125 pounds. These do not include the weights of experiments.

Electrical power and distribution for Spacelab will be provided by the Shuttle Orbiter's fuel cell power system. Additional power will be provided by the pallet's power system if required. Spacelab does have an emergency independent power source.

Atmosphere for Spacelab will be provided by equipment on each module which will enable scientists to work in an oxygen/nitrogen atmosphere similar to that which exists at sea level. Communications with the ground are provided through the Orbiter's systems.

Spacelab

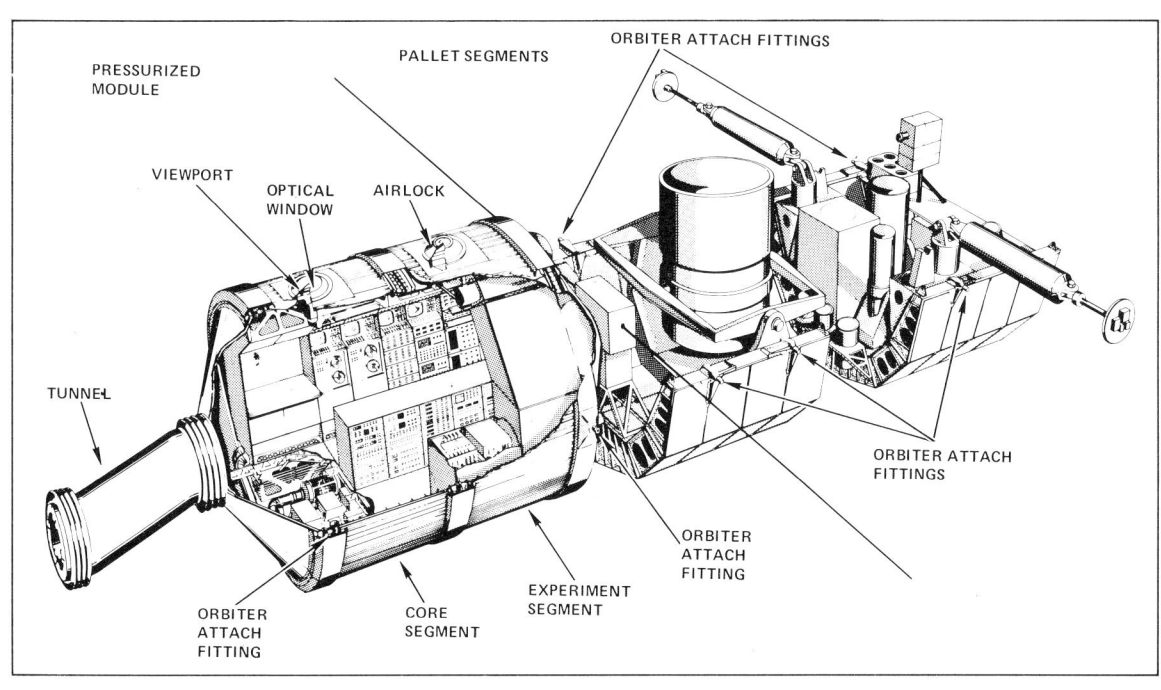

Spacelab in Earth orbit – cutaway showing artist's concept of astronauts about various tasks. One is working outside the vehicle in the cargo bay, one is working in the laboratory and another is returning to the Orbiter cabin through the pressurised tunnel.

Scientist astronauts flying in Spacelab will eat and sleep in the Orbiter and not in Spacelab itself.

Spacelab cannot fly independently of the Shuttle. On later missions, however, this may be possible as a result of modifications.

NASA will use Spacelab components to carry out its own missions. Indeed, of the 725 Shuttle missions planned up to 1994, 160 will use Spacelab. Not all of these missions will be flown for European experiments and by European astronauts. Only one European will fly on Spacelab 1. Ten Europeans will have taken flights by 1990, maybe up to four of them together on one mission.

In order to train payload specialists in the art of working in Spacelab, an aircraft was kitted out like the space station and flown on missions called ASSESS. This stands for Airborne Science Spacelab Experiment System Simulation. Fifteen Assess flights lasting six hours were flown in a four-engine jet called Galileo 2.

For Assess, equipment and experiments resembling those to be used in Spacelab were installed in Galileo. In addition, a mobile van parked next to the aircraft after each flight was used for living quarters. The payload specialists spent their off-duty time in the van, thus simulating the complete isolation involved in a space mission.

During the Assess flights, payload specialists conducted actual scientific experiments such as surveying Earth's resources, atmospheric pollution monitoring and infra-red astronomy.

Spacelab is expected to make significant contributions to science, medicine, industrial processing and many other valuable fields. In perspective, however, the most important result of the international space laboratory may well be the great step forward that it represents towards global co-operation in space. It is an outstanding example of how peoples of many lands can unite their talents and resources in future space projects to benefit the whole of humanity.

THE SPACE SHUTTLE BASES

Cape Canaveral, the Kennedy Space Center, Vandenburg, Edwards, Downey, Palmdale, Bay St. Louis. These locations, and many others spread across the United States, are all important links in the chain of Space Shuttle operations.

The Shuttle Orbiter is built by the Space Division of the Rockwell International Corporation in Downey, California. Rockwell is responsible to the American space agency, NASA, in Houston, Texas, for the design, development, testing and evaluation of the Orbiter. The final assembly, testing and check-out of the Orbiter takes place at Palmdale, California, in facilities provided by the United States Air Force.

The design, development, manufacture, testing and assembly of the Space Shuttle main engines is handled by the Rocketdyne Division of Rockwell at Canoga Park, California. This Division is responsible to NASA's Marshall Space Flight Center who, at Huntsville, Alabama, manage the development of all the major components of the Space Shuttle system.

The external tank is developed at the Michoud Facility in Louisiana of the Martin Marietta Company, which is also responsible to the Marshall Space Flight Center.

Thiokol Chemical Corporation in Brigham City, Utah, makes the motors of the solid rocket boosters. These are returned to this company for refurbishment after their recovery from the sea after launch. Thiokol is also responsible to the Marshall Space Flight Center.

The structures of the solid rocket boosters are manufactured by McDonnell-Douglas Astronautics at Huntingdon Beach, California, while United Space Boosters Incorporated at Sunnyvale, California, check out and assemble the boosters.

Over one hundred companies produce the other components of the Shuttle system: such things as general-purpose wire, transducers, water coolers, heat-resistant materials, toggle switches and regulators. These companies deliver the components to Rockwell

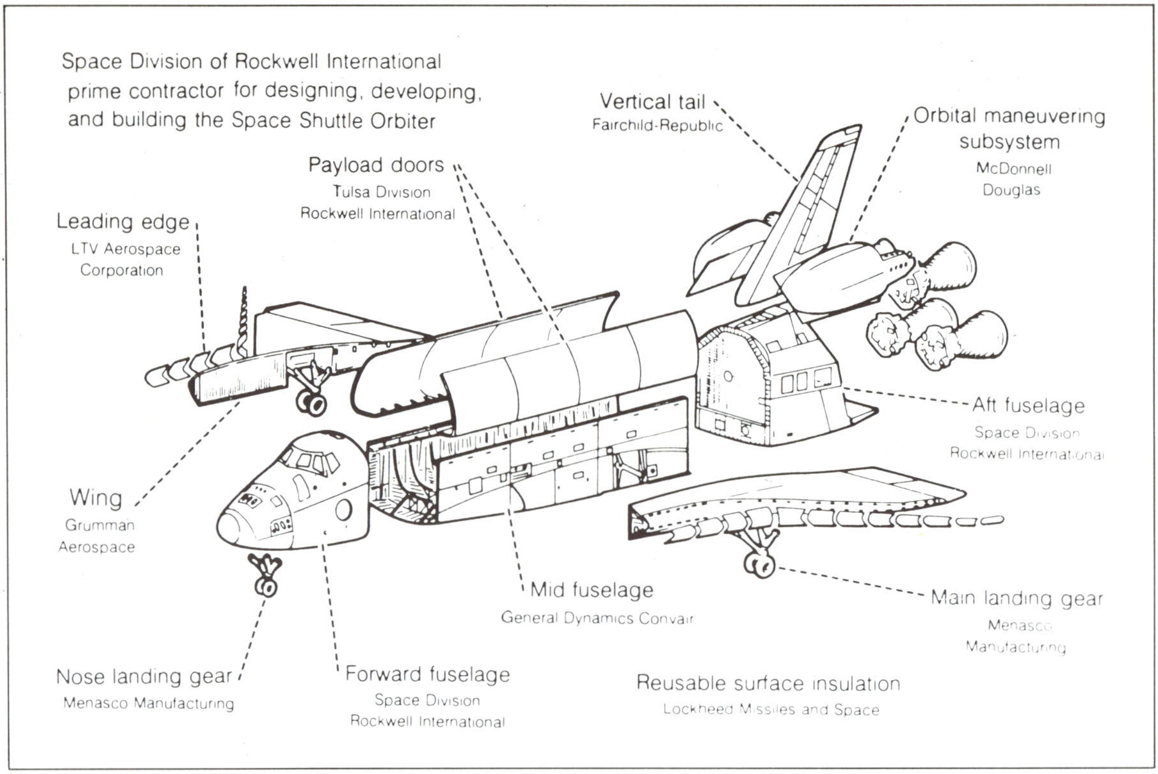

Space Division of Rockwell International
prime contractor for designing, developing,
and building the Space Shuttle Orbiter

Vertical tail
Fairchild-Republic

Orbital maneuvering
subsystem
McDonnell
Douglas

Payload doors
Tulsa Division
Rockwell International

Leading edge
LTV Aerospace
Corporation

Aft fuselage
Space Division
Rockwell International

Wing
Grumman
Aerospace

Mid fuselage
General Dynamics Convair

Main landing gear
Menasco
Manufacturing

Nose landing gear
Menasco Manufacturing

Forward fuselage
Space Division
Rockwell International

Reusable surface insulation
Lockheed Missiles and Space

*How different companies
are responsible for
building different
components of the
Shuttle Orbiter.*

*The National Space
Technology Laboratory at
Bay St Louis, Missouri,
where the main engines
are tested.*

*Above – static firing of
the Shuttle main engine
at Bay St Louis.*

*Above left – Shuttle
assembled for vibration
test at the Marshall
Space Flight Center,
Alabama.*

*Left – preparations at
Thiokol Chemical
Corporation in Utah for
a test firing of a solid
rocket booster.*

and other major contractors of the Shuttle for integration into the system.

Testing of the orbital manoeuvering system and reaction control system engines takes place at NASA's White Sands Test Facility in New Mexico. Holloman Air Force Base in New Mexico is utilised for escape system tests. The escape system equipment provides the testing of the Orbiter ejection panels and ejection seats that were provided for the commander and pilot of the ALT flights in Orbiter 101 and which will be used for the initial flights of Orbiter 102.

The National Space Technology Laboratory of Bay St. Louis, Missouri, is used for the testing of the Shuttle main engines.

Vandenburg Air Force Base in California is the site from where the Space Shuttle will be launched into polar orbit. The Shuttle will be launched down the Pacific Missile Range in a southerly direction, over the South Pole. Some of the Shuttle flights from Vandenburg will be made by NASA but most will be military missions, carried out by the US Department of Defense. The Shuttle facilities at Vandenburg are provided by the US Department of Defense, including a special launch pad and a 15,000-feet concrete runway. Vandenburg has been an important military space base since 1959, when the first military satellite, Discoverer 1, was launched from there.

The first flights of Orbiter 101 were made during Approach and Landing Tests at the NASA Hugh L. Dryden Research Center at the USAF Edwards Air Force Base in California's Mojave Desert. Landings of the first Shuttle Orbiter space flights will also be made here. Edwards is one of the most famous air bases in the world. It was from here that Man first broke the sound barrier when Chuck Yeager flew the X-1 experimental rocket plane in October 1947. Rocket planes and many other experimental aircraft have been tested at Edwards, including the legendary X-15 rocket plane that test pilot Joe Walker flew 67 miles into space in 1966 and William Knight flew at six times the speed of sound during a flight in 1967.

Houston in Texas is also a legendary name, being the flight control centre for the Apollo moonflights. Houston is the home of the NASA Lyndon B. Johnson Space Center where the astronauts are based and trained and from where Shuttle flights will be monitored and controlled. The first time Houston was used as a manned flight control centre was in 1965 when Gemini 4 was launched, and since then all flights have been carefully watched over by men at rows of consoles monitoring the performance of all the components and systems in manned spacecraft.

The most well-known space base in the world is Cape Canaveral, from where the first and most of the Space Shuttles will be launched. Cape Canaveral is actually a little south of the Shuttle launch pads, which are situated at the Kennedy Space Center on Merritt Island. The history of the Cape goes back a long way.

Picture a lush, sub-tropical peninsula of sand jutting out into the Caribbean-warmed Atlantic Ocean – a desolate expanse of sand, snarled brush and palmetto scrub, inhabited by alligators, snakes and many species of birds and hordes of voracious mosquitoes: you may not think of this as a place you would associate with the space race. This however is Cape Canaveral.

The Cape's state, Florida, was discovered for the Old World by one of Christopher Columbus's sea captains named Juan de Leon in 1509. If ever he landed at this desolate site, he surely wouldn't have stayed long. Not only was the Cape inhabited by the insects and reptiles but also occupied by Red Indians.

These inhabitants of the Cape remained virtually undisturbed through three more centuries under Spanish, French and British control until just after the American Civil War, when the town of Cocoa was established in 1868 and a lighthouse was built at the tip of the Cape. It is a landmark that remains to this day, surrounded by gantry towers – modern-day reminders that the Cape is now a spaceport.

First construction work on the Cape began with the building of a temporary blockhouse for a launch facility for rockets on 9 May, 1950. The first launch pad was built by 15 June. The rockets were German V-2 missiles captured at the end of the Second World War and converted to accept a second stage called Corporal. The first rocket launch from Cape Canaveral took place on 24 July, 1950, when the 'Bumper 8' rocket rose ponderously from the scrub-surrounded launch pad watched by about five news and cameramen. Nineteen years later, almost to the day, 3400 newsmen from all over the world witnessed another great milestone when the manned Apollo 11 left for the Moon.

Today, Cape Canaveral and the NASA Kennedy Space Center is a mass of sprawling launch pads, concrete roads, and buildings covering a very wide area on a strip of land about 15 miles long. Some launch pads are now unused, such as Pad 14 where John Glenn took off to become the first American in orbit and Pad 19 from where the Geminis took off. But many still are in use, such as the Titan 3C/Centaur complex, a Delta launch pad and an Atlas Centaur pad.

In the 80s though, the Cape will be known as the Shuttle Spaceport. Many of the facilities that were used for the Apollo programme are being used again for the Shuttle. These include the Vertical Assembly Building, the VAB, which is so large that clouds form on the ceiling; the crawler transporters which take the Shuttle from the VAB to the launch site; and the launch complex, Pad 39A.

One new development has been the building of one of the world's largest concrete runways, called the Orbiter landing facility. It is about three miles long and 300 feet wide, and has a further 1000-feet safety overrun at each end. The landing facility also includes a microwave landing system which guides the Orbiter in to make an automatic landing.

A 'mate-demate' facility enables the Shuttle Orbiter's removal from a Boeing jumbo jet carrier aircraft should the Orbiter come to

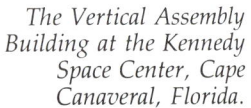

The Vertical Assembly Building at the Kennedy Space Center, Cape Canaveral, Florida.

the Cape this way from Edwards or Vandenburg, or should it need to be ferried to Vandenburg.

There is also an Orbiter processing facility. This is located next to the VAB. It is connected to the landing facility by a two-mile long toway on which the Shuttle travels after making its landing. The processing facility is a kind of aircraft hangar in sterilised 'white-room' conditions, where residual fuels left over in the Orbiter are rendered safe, flight and landing systems are refurbished and payloads are removed or installed.

Remaining Shuttle facilities at the Kennedy Space Center are modifications to existing facilities originally designed and built to support Apollo.

Mobile launchers on which Saturn 5/Apollo rockets moved from the VAB to the launch pad have been modified to take the complete Space Shuttle system. The Shuttle actually uses these launchers as launch pads. The launchers are placed on an enormous concrete launching area at Pad 39A. A flame trench lies directly beneath three holes in the launcher through which flame from the Shuttle's main engine and the two solid fuel rockets gushes out. The flame hits the trench and is deflected with great force out of either side of the launch pad.

The launchers are taken to the launch pad from the VAB by

Pad 39 at Cape Canaveral, from where the Shuttle is launched.

crawler transporters, with giant tank-like wheels, that move the crawler along at two mph.

Inside the VAB, the Shuttle's components are linked carefully together to form flight-ready models. Two of the four high bays in which completed Saturn rockets were built have been modified to build the Shuttle while the other two are used to store the external tanks and the solid rocket boosters.

Firing rooms 1 and 2 of the Apollo launch control centre, the 'brain' of the complex, are fitted with equipment making possible the highly automated Space Shuttle launch sequence called the launch processing system. This system requires only about one tenth of the manpower needed to launch Apollo – 45 as compared to 450. The final countdown for a Shuttle launch requires about two and a half hours instead of the 28 hours needed for the final countdown of an Apollo/Saturn vehicle.

Major changes made to launch Pad 39A, from where the Shuttle departs, include the building of a fixed Shuttle service access tower which contains the payload change-out room or PCR. The PCR provides the capability of loading and unloading payloads at the launch pad. It is a 'white-room' mounted on a semi-circular track extending from the Shuttle service and access tower and is retracted to its park site before launch. The pad also includes a water sound suppression system which emits thousands of gallons of water on to the pad at lift-off to protect the Shuttle crew and pay-loads from acoustical damage and the pad from the heat.

Other areas of Shuttle operation at the Cape include the hypergol maintenance facility, which is used to test and check out the Orbiter's propulsion system and forward reaction control system after each mission. These systems use highly toxic propel-lants which ignite on contact with each other. They are called hypergolic propellants.

An operations and check-out building for the Spacelab space station has been built in the VAB. A parachute facility handles the 'chutes of the solid rocket boosters. This facility washes, dries, stores and packs the parachutes for reuse.

A spacecraft vertical and processing facility permits the check-out, processing and integration of the Shuttle's cargoes prior to installation in the Shuttle payload bay on the launch pad.

A receiving and disassembly site for the solid rocket boosters, called the solid rocket booster recovery and disassembly facility, has also been built.

The eventual cost of turning Cape Canaveral into the Shuttle Spaceport has been about £400 million. During the 1980s it is going to be a very busy place indeed.

TESTING THE SHUTTLE 5

Before committing the Shuttle Orbiter to a flight into space, it was necessary to test fly it in the Earth's atmosphere. Scientists wanted to ensure that the Orbiter would be able to fly like an aircraft and land safely. Its landing speed was higher than that of a conventional aircraft. A scheme was established to fly the Shuttle Orbiter on the top of the fuselage of a modified Boeing 747 jumbo jet and free it from the jet thousands of feet up, allowing it to fly down and land.

This flight plan was called the Approach and Landing Test, or ALT for short. A number of flights were planned involving the use of different flight profiles and approach angles to the runway. The ALT free-flight test programme was designed to enable pilots to get experience of actually guiding the Shuttle glider and landing it. ALT was also to test automatic approach and landings. These were attempted using computer-based equipment on the ground and in the cockpit of the Shuttle.

Four astronauts were chosen in two teams, each having a commander and a pilot, to carry out the ALT programme. They included a civilian test pilot who was scheduled to become the sixth man on the Moon until his spacecraft, Apollo 13, exploded in 1970. His name is Fred Haise. His pilot in ALT was Lt. Col. Gordon Fullerton, USAF, who had not flown into space. The second team was commanded by Colonel Joe Engle, USAF, who had flown three times into space in the X-15 rocket plane. His pilot was US Navy Commander Dick Truly.

The Shuttle Orbiter was rolled out of the factory of Rockwell International in Palmdale, California, on 17 September 1976. Called Enterprise, after the spacecraft of the *Star Trek* television series, this Shuttle was designated No. 101 the first of five Shuttle Orbiters to be built.

Enterprise was taken by road to Edwards Air Force Base in California on 31 January 1977 and was mated to the specially converted Boeing 747 the following month. Flight testing moved gingerly forward. First, the mated combination of Shuttle and

jumbo jet carried out taxi tests on the runway, then, on 18 February 1977, the Enterprise was airborne at last, though still attached to the jumbo jet throughout a test that was called an 'unmanned inert captive flight'.

Four of these flights followed before men flew on the Enterprise. These were for captive tests too – with the Shuttle still attached to the jumbo. They were called 'manned captive flights'. Astronauts Fred Haise and Gordon Fullerton made the first manned captive flight on 18 June 1977.

There then followed two more captive flights before the big day of Enterprise's first free flight came on 12 August 1977.

In order to separate from the jumbo jet, the Shuttle Orbiter Enterprise was placed on the jumbo's fuselage with a nose-up attitude of six degrees, so that when the separation mechanisms were released the airstream would provide the lift required to separate the two craft.

On 12 August the Enterprise, weighing 556,000 pounds, was sitting on top of the Boeing jumbo jet as it screamed down the runway at Edwards Air Force Base in California and heaved itself into the air. At the controls of the jumbo was British-born Fitzroy Fulton.

Fulton flew the combination to a height of 28,000 feet and

cruised at that altitude while the Shuttle pilots Haise and Fullerton, inside the Orbiter, carried out various systems checks. Fulton then reduced the height by about four thousand feet. At 8 hours 48 minutes 30 seconds in the morning, Pacific Daylight time, Fred Haise and Gordon Fullerton became the first pilots of the Shuttle as the Enterprise sprang clear of the jumbo and silently began its free fall towards Edwards.

Haise and Fullerton rolled the craft 20° to the right in order to complete a safe separation from the jumbo, then pitched down the nose of the giant glider and accelerated, turning the craft twice through 90° in order to face it towards the Edwards runway. The Shuttle then began approaching the runway. The undercarriage was deployed at 180 feet and the main gear hit the runway at a speed of 212 mph. The Shuttle gradually slowed down, travelling 11,000 feet before coming to a complete standstill at the end of the

The Shuttle Orbiter with 'cone-on' during an early ALT flight.

flight which had lasted five minutes, 21 seconds. Fred Haise called the flight 'super slick' and Fullerton called the Shuttle a 'very stable airplane'.

The first flight was a dramatic success. Joe Engle and Dick Truly took turns to pilot the Enterprise during the second and their first free flight on 13 September 1977. This ALT 2 mission lasted five minutes, 28 seconds. The Enterprise was separated at 26,000 feet and hit the runway at 218 mph after a flight that performed a different set of manoeuvres. During the flight Joe Engle reported that the Shuttle was 'performing superbly' and Dick Truly said that he thought it was 'an excellent handling flying machine'.

A five-minute, 34-second flight followed on 23 September, piloted by Haise and Fullerton. This time, when the main gear hit the runway the landing speed was 219 mph and by the time the nose wheel touched down the speed had been reduced to 179 mph.

With these three flights completed, the manager of the ALT programme, veteran astronaut Donald 'Deke' Slayton, decided to move on to the next phase, which would involve flying the Shuttle just as it would look as it returned to Earth from orbit, with the three Shuttle main engines and two orbital manoeuvring system nozzles on the tail open to the elements. For the earlier ALT flights these were covered with a cone-shaped structure.

The first 'cone-off' flight, as it was called, was made by Joe Engle and Dick Truly. The Enterprise separated from the jumbo jet at 22,000 feet on 12 October 1977. Lasting only two minutes, 34 seconds, this flight ended with a landing at 217 mph. The craft came to a complete stop at 5,725 feet. The flight path into Edwards was much steeper than on previous flights and this enabled the astronauts to evaluate the handling characteristics of the Shuttle on an unusual flight path. After the flight Truly said that the Enterprise was a 'great machine (that) flies good'. He also said that the handling of the vehicle was similar to previous flights with the cone on the tail, except that rate of deceleration was reduced and speed decreased due to increased drag by the airstream on the tail engine structure.

The final flight of the ALT programme was made by astronauts Haise and Fullerton. This flight took place on 26 October 1977. The landing of the Shuttle was witnessed by His Royal Highness the Prince of Wales, Prince Charles, who was on an official visit to the United States at the time. It wasn't a very good landing. The vehicle bounced twice and lurched a little sideways before becoming stable. Previously the Shuttle had landed on a dry lake-bed runway, but this time the vehicle landed on the main concrete runway at

Edwards. Haise picks up the story, 'the landing seemed as smooth *Orbiter Enterprise in* as previous flights but after that I was caught by surprise and all at *flight.* once I found myself in the air again. This time it skipped . . . . Gordon (Fullerton) told me to let go of my stick and the bouncing stopped'.

The Shuttle came to a stop well within the 15,000-feet length planned for the runways at Cape Canaveral and Vandenburg where the vehicle will be making landings at the end of its operational missions.

After this flight the Shuttle was pronounced fit to fly in space. The Shuttle was remated to the modified jumbo jet for a series of four 'ferry' flight tests during which the vehicles simulated the flight that would be made between Edwards Air Force Base and Cape Canaveral at the end of each early orbital test flight. One flight lasted four hours, 17 minutes.

Ferry flights will also be made should the Shuttle make an emergency landing elsewhere in the world and need to return to base for launching. For example, military flights of the Shuttle will make emergency landings at Hickman Air Force Base in Hawaii, if necessary, and a ferry flight would be made from there to Vandenburg.

After the ferry flights the Shuttle 101 was taken to the Marshall Space Flight Center in Alabama, where the vehicle was mated to

Orbiter Enterprise separates from its 747 carrier aircraft at 22,000 feet during the first 'cone-off' test flight, October 1977.

Orbiter Enterprise lands at Edwards Air Base at the end of an ALT flight.

the external tank and solid rocket boosters for a series of structural tests simulating the vibration that would be experienced at lift-off and during flight. The tests took place in 1978, at the same time that the Shuttle engines were tested.

THE SHUTTLENAUTS

When the Space Shuttle flies operationally, four types of astronauts will fly in it. There will be a commander, a pilot, mission specialists and payload scientists or specialists. The commanders, pilots and mission specialists will all be selected from the 62 astronauts in training at NASA's Manned Spacecraft Center in Houston. Thirty-five of these astronauts have only recently been chosen and are unlikely to make flights until all of the remaining 27 trained and operational astronauts have flown on missions.

Of these 27, nine are already picked for missions, seven as commanders and pilots on the first orbital tests and two as mission specialists on the first Spacelab flight.

The remaining 18 comprise eight scientist astronauts waiting to be assigned mission specialist positions and ten pilot astronauts due to be assigned as commanders and pilots.

. Eleven of the 27 due to make the first missions have got space-flight experience and two have walked on the moon.

Payload scientists are different. They will be chosen to fly on Spacelab missions and other flights to operate specific experiment packages. So far, nine people are in line for flights in Spacelabs 1 and 2, only six of whom will fly, four on Spacelab 2 and two on Spacelab 1, one of whom will be the first Western European in orbit.

The payload specialists will not undergo any special training, other than intensive nine months pre-flight briefing. They are in effect in for the ride, not having any responsibility for actually flying the mission, just operating the experiments once the Shuttle is in orbit.

Of the 62 NASA astronauts in line for Shuttle assignments, 30 are potential mission specialists and 32 are in the commander and pilot pool.

These are the pilot-astronauts, in alphabetical order:

Alan Bean

The first is one of the most experienced: **Alan Bean**, the former US Navy (USN) Captain who was the fourth man to walk on the moon. Bean, who has not yet been assigned a flight, is likely to command the Spacelab 1 mission. He was selected in the third group of astronauts, chosen in October 1963, and served as Gemini 10 back-up command pilot before being selected for the Apollo 9 back-up crew, which put him in line for Apollo 12 and a flight to the Moon in November 1969. Bean then flew Skylab 3 in 1973, remaining in the space station for 59 days. Together with his moon-walking experience, he has 10 hours, 26 minutes space-walking time under his belt out of his 1,671 hours, 45 minutes spaceflight travelling time. Alan Bean is now a civilian with NASA, and served as the back-up commander of the Apollo-Soyuz test project flight (ASTP) in 1975, during which an Apollo spacecraft docked with a Russian Soyuz in orbit for a joint mission.

Colonel Karol J. Bobko, USAF, was originally selected to pilot the United States Air Force's Manned Orbital Laboratory (MOL) until the programme was cancelled in 1969. He joined NASA in the seventh astronaut corps in August 1969 and took part in a 56-day simulation of a Skylab flight and was also a support crew member of the Apollo-Soyuz

ASTP team. He still awaits a spaceflight after over ten years in training.

Vance de Voe Brand is a civilian test pilot who was one of 19 Class 5 astronauts chosen by NASA in 1966. He waited until 1975 before he made a spaceflight as command module pilot of Apollo 18, the ASTP flight, during which he clocked up 217 hours 28 minutes of space experience. Along the way through to ASTP he served as support crewman on Apollo 8 and 13 and was back-up command module pilot of Apollo 15 and back-up commander of Skylabs 3 and 4, as well as stand-by Skylab Rescue flight commander. Brand is one of seven astronauts chosen to fly on one of the Shuttle orbital flight tests (STS, standing for Space Transportation System). He commands a two-man crew comprising himself and Gordon Fullerton.

One of the new batch of pilots in the Group 8 NASA astronauts chosen in 1978 is **Lt. Cdr. Daniel 'Dan' C. Brandenstein**, USN. Like the other 34 recruits in Class 8, he will not be placed on flight status until 1981.

Three more Class 8 pilot astronaut candidates are **Lt. Cdr. Michael L. Coats**, USN, **Richard 'Dick' O. Covey** a USAF Major, and **Lt. Cdr. John O. Creighton.**

The pilot of the first orbital flight test (STS 1) of the Space Shuttle is **Cdr. Robert L. Crippen**, USN. He is the first of the seven

Vance Brand

Manned Orbital Laboratory programme pilots who were transferred to NASA in 1969 to be assigned to a flight. Crippen took part in the 56-day simulation of a Skylab flight and served in the support crew of Skylab 2 and 3 and Apollo 18, the ASTP mission. Crippen flies STS 1 with John Young.

Space Transportation System 1's back-up commander and a commander of a later STS test flight is **Colonel Joe Henry Engle** of the US Air Force, who, as pilot of the X-15 rocket plane, flew three times over an altitude of 50 miles which qualified him for astronaut's wings. After joining the NASA Group 5 astronaut corps in 1966, Engle waited until 1971 for a flight assignment as back-up lunar module pilot of Apollo 14, qualifying him for the job he would have performed on Apollo 17, becoming the twelfth man on the Moon, had not budget cuts meant him being replaced on this the last moon flight by geologist Jack Schmitt. Engle was commander of one of the two crews who flew the Approach and Landing Tests in 1977. He flew on the second and fourth ALT flights with the man who will be his pilot on the STS flight, Dick Truly, and they were the first team to fly the Orbiter 'cone-off'.

ALT crews – left to right: Gordon Fullerton, Fred Haise, Joe Engle and Dick Truly. Haise has since resigned from NASA.

Another man who flew ALT missions, as pilot to Fred Haise, was **Lt. Col. Charles Gordon Fullerton**, USAF, who is pilot to Vance Brand on an early STS test mission. Fullerton is an ex-MOL astronaut, one of Class 7 who joined NASA in 1969. Before making three ALT flights, Fullerton was a support crew member of the Apollo 14 and 17 missions.

Gordon Fullerton

Joe Engle

Lt. Robert 'Hoot' L. Gibson, USN, **Major Fred D. Gregory**, USAF, and civilian test pilot **Stanley D. 'Dave' Griggs** are all Class 8 pilot astronaut candidates.

Fred Haise, who was to have been commander of an early STS test flight, has recently resigned from NASA after 142 hours, 54 minutes of space experience. He became the first man to fly the Shuttle Orbiter during the first of his ALT flights in 1977. A civilian test pilot who joined NASA with Group 5 in 1966, Haise was lucky to survive the explosion of Apollo 13 in 1970. Had that mission been successful, he would have been the sixth man to land on the Moon. He also served as Apollo 8 back-up lunar module pilot, Buzz Aldrin's back-up on Apollo 11, and back-up commander of Apollo 16.

Robert Crippen

Former USAF Colonel, **Henry W. Hartsfield Jr.**, is a Class 7 MOL pilot who served on the support crews of Apollo 16 and Skylabs 2, 3 and 4. He is awaiting assignment, probably as pilot of a later Shuttle crew.

Jack Lousma

Executive officer with Squadron 145, **Cdr. Frederick 'Rick' Hauck**, USN, is one of the new pilot astronaut candidates who will probably pilot the Shuttle after 1982.

Another man scheduled to fly an STS test Mission as pilot is **Lt. Col. Jack R. Lousma** of the US Marines who gained 1,427 hours 9 minutes (11 hours 2 minutes of it space-walking) space-flight experience on the Skylab 3 flight in 1973. Lousma joined the NASA astronaut corps in 1966 and served on the support crews of Apollo 9, 10 and 13 and was also back-up docking module pilot of Apollo 18, the ASTP flight.

Thomas Ken Mattingly II, a Commander in the US Navy was scheduled to fly Apollo 13 as command module pilot in April 1970 when, three days before the flight, he was replaced by Jack Swigert, because he had been exposed to German measles. So, Mattingly escaped the Apollo 13 drama. He flew on Apollo 16, also as command module pilot, making a space walk lasting 1 hour, 13 minutes in between the Moon and Earth during the return journey of the mission, which lasted 265 hours 51 minutes. An astronaut chosen with the fifth group in 1966, Mattingly was also support crew member of the Apollo 8 and 11 missions.

One of the new astronaut candidates is **Lt. Cdr. Jon McBride**, USN.

Probably the unluckiest of the 19 Class 5 astronauts is **Bruce McCandless** a USN Commander who is still waiting for an assignment after being in training since 1966. He has been passed over many times and has seen astronauts of later groups assigned above him. He was support crew member of Apollo 14 and back-up pilot of the first Skylab flight. His main area of expertise is in the development of spacesuits and astronaut manoeuvring units, which perhaps he may get an opportunity to test fly as pilot on a later Shuttle flight.

USAF **Captain Steven R. Nagel**, a former test pilot at Edwards Air Force Base, is another new astronaut chosen in 1978.

Marine **Lt. Col. Robert F. Overmyer** and USAF **Colonel Donald H. Peterson** are two of the seven MOL pilots who joined NASA in 1969. Overmyer was an Apollo 17 and 18 (ASTP) support crew member and Peterson served on Apollo 16 in the same capacity.

Skylab 4's **Bill Pogue**, a USAF Lieutenant Colonel, stayed in space for 84 days in 1973 and '74 then left NASA, although he is available for assignment to Shuttle flights.

Three more new pilot astronauts are **Major Francis R. 'Dick' Scobee**, USAF, **Captain Brewster H. Shaw Jr.**, USAF, and **Captain Loren J. Shriver**, USAF, all former test pilots at Edwards Air Force Base.

Surely the most remarkable

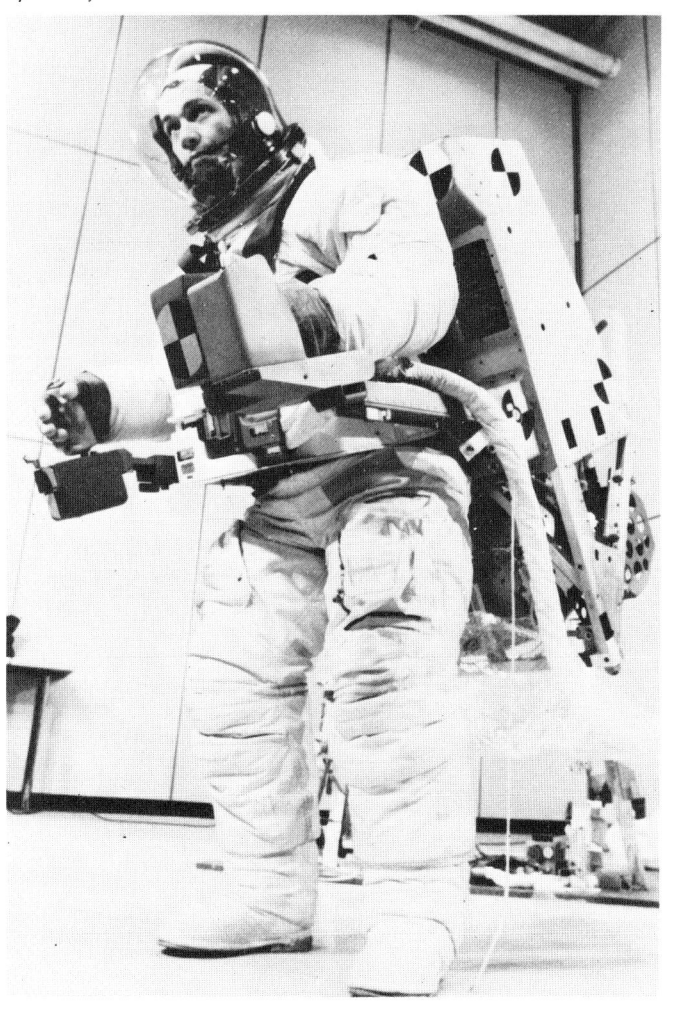

Bruce McCandless, wearing a jet-powered backpack which allows an astronaut to work untethered for up to 30 minutes outside his spacecraft.

Shuttle Mission Simulator used for training Shuttle crews at the Johnson Space Center, Houston, Texas.

man in the astronaut corps is **Donald K. 'Deke' Slayton** who has been in NASA's astronaut group for twenty years. He was one of the original 'Mercury Seven' astronauts and was scheduled to become the sixth man in space in May 1962 when doctors dropped him from the planned flight and from astronaut status because of a 'heart flutter'. It took Slayton ten years to change the doctors' minds and by this time the Apollo programme had ended. All that was left was ASTP so he got on board that flight as docking module pilot at the ripe old age of 51. He has 217 hours 28 minutes space experience and is currently manager of the STS test flight programme. He could very well take command of a later Shuttle flight.

A member of the early STS flight test crews as back-up pilot on STS 1 is **Dick Truly**, a Commander in the USN. An ex-MOL astronaut, Truly was also pilot to Joe Engle during two of the five ALT flights in 1977. Truly was a support crew member of all three Skylab flights and ASTP.

Dave H. Walker and **'Dan' E. Williams** both USN Lieutenant Commanders, are two more new pilots.

Former Navy Captain **Paul J. Weitz**, pronounced 'Whites', was a 1966 NASA astronaut. He served on Apollo 12 as support crew member before being selected for the first Skylab flight which he flew for 672 hours 49 minutes.

Finally, at the end of the list of pilots and commanders in the NASA Shuttle group, is the first Space Shuttle commander and one of the most experienced American spacemen. STS 1 Commander **John W. Young**, a former Navy Captain, joined the NASA astronaut corps with eight other spacemen, including such legendary names as Frank Borman and Neil Armstrong, in 1962. He flew the first Gemini spacecraft as pilot to Gus Grissom in 1965, flew Gemini 10 as commander in 1966, Apollo 10 around the Moon as command module pilot in 1969, and walked on the Moon during the Apollo 16 mission in 1972 which he commanded. He was also back-up Gemini 6 pilot, back-up Apollo 7 command module pilot and back-up commander of Apollo 13 and 17. Young was Chief of the Astronaut Office until his assignment to STS 1 and has 533 hours, 33 minutes space experience, including 20 hours, 15 minutes moon-walking. STS 1 makes Young the first man to make five spaceflights.

Paul Weitz
Dick Truly

John Young wearing
a Shuttle spacesuit.

The Mission Specialists will also come from the NASA astronaut corps, which includes scientists. They will be responsible for monitoring Shuttle flight systems and experiments and will perform major science tasks in flight representing medical, biological, earth sciences, physical and chemical sciences and engineering disciplines.

There are 30 Mission Specialists in the Group, three of whom have space flight experience as science pilots of Skylab:

Joseph Allen joined the second group of NASA astro-scientists in 1967 with Group 6. He served as ground-based mission scientist on Apollo 15 before taking leave of absence. He is available to make Shuttle flights should he be called upon to do so by NASA.

Five new science astronauts in the Group 8 class are **Major Guion 'Guy' S. Bluford Jr.**, USAF, PhD., an aerospace engineer; Marine **Captain Jim F. Buchli**, an aeronautical engineer; **Major John M. Fabian**, USAF, PhD, assistant professor of aeronautics at the USAF academy; **Dr. Anna Fisher**, one of six women in the Class 8 corps; and aeronautical engineer **Lt. Dale A. Gardner**, USN.

One of Spacelab 1's mission specialists will be **Dr. Owen Garriott** who joined NASA in 1965 with six other astro-scientists in Group 4 and had to wait a long time for a mission assignment as science pilot of Skylab 3, during which he spent 1,427 hours, 9 minutes in space and 13 hours, 43 minutes space-walking.

Another of that Class 4 astronaut group was **Dr. Edward Gibson,** who flew in Skylab 4 for 84 days, performing space walks lasting 15 hours, 17 minutes. He will be a mission specialist on an early operational Shuttle flight.

Mechanical engineer **Terry J. Hart** and astronomer **Steve Hawley** are two new recruits to the astronaut corps.

Astronomer **Karl G. Henize** joined NASA in 1967 and worked on a number of experiments for Gemini and Skylab. He is still waiting for a flight assignment.

Another astronomer is **Jeff Hoffman**, a Class 8 astronaut-candidate who will be ready for a flight in 1981.

Navy doctor **Captain Joseph P. Kerwin** was one of the first NASA astro-scientists. He flew Skylab 2 in 1973, clocking up 672 hours, 49 minutes space experience. He is likely to make an early Shuttle flight.

Electrical engineer **William B. Lenoir** joined NASA in 1967 and served as back-up science pilot on Skylab 3 and 4. Test pilot and nuclear physicist **Don Lind** also served on Skylab back-up crews.

Lind joined the NASA astronaut corps in 1966 but opted to become a science astronaut rather than a pilot astronaut.

Another woman in the new astronaut group is **Shannon W. Lucid**, a biochemist. She is joined by physicist **Ron E. McNair** and aeronautical engineer **Richard M. 'Mike' Mullane**, a Captain in the US Air Force.

Dr. Story Musgrave is one of the 1967 group. He was back-up science pilot for Skylab 2.

Astronomer **George Nelson** and Hawaiian USAF Captain and aerospace engineer **Ellison 'El' S. Onizuka** are two new astronauts.

Astronomer **Robert Allan Ridley Parker** will be the second mission specialist on Spacelab 1. He joined NASA in the 1967 group of astronauts and served on the support crews of Apollo 15 and 17 and as programme scientist for Skylab.

Dr. William Edgar Thornton comes from the same group. He was the science pilot of the 56-day Skylab simulation and served on the support crew of Skylab 2, 3 and 4.

Joseph Kerwin

The final seven members of the Mission Specialists branch of NASA's astronaut corps are all new astronauts: **Judy Resnik**, an electrical engineer, physicist **Sally Ride**, physician **Margaret 'Rhea' Seddon**, US Army aerospace engineer **Major Robert Stewart**, geologist **Kathy Sullivan**, Doctor **'Norm' Thagard** and engineer **Jim D. van Hoften**.

The payload specialists from whom two will be chosen to take the nine-month training for Spacelab 1 are **Michael L. Lampton**, an American space physicist, **Byron Lichtenberg**, an American doctor and three European candidates, scientist **Ulf Merbold** from Germany, astronomer **Claude Nicollier** and physicist **Wubbo Ockels** of Holland.

Six woman scientists recruited for astronaut training in 1978: clockwise from top left – Dr Anna Fisher, Shannon Lucid, biochemist, Judy Resnik, electrical engineer, Sally Ride, physicist, Rhea Seddon, a doctor, and geologist Kathy Sullivan.

Astronaut training is highly involved and time-consuming. At Houston the astronauts attend classes to learn all there is to know about spaceflight, spacecraft, celestial mechanics, and all the other associated subjects. They 'fly' the centrifuge, used to simulate the forces of acceleration and deceleration. At another location they simulate weightlessness in a neutral buoyancy tank, where they learn about space-walking and practise the tasks they will have to perform in space. The astronauts visit many locations all over the United States, flying their own T38 jets to attend various meetings involved in spacecraft development and mission plans.

Once selected, the astronaut spends most of his time in the Shuttle simulator practising the flight to the last degree. He also practises Shuttle flying characteristics in a converted Convair jet plane.

In space, the astronaut wears a spacesuit during times of high risk – for example launch and re-entry and, of course, for space walks. Previously, the spacesuits were purpose-built for each astronaut but now they are manufactured 'off-the-peg' in large, medium and small sizes. An astronaut manoeuvring unit is being developed for space walks.

By the time they make a space-flight the astronauts have 'flown' the mission many times in simulators and know about every nut and bolt aboard their spacecraft.

ASTRONAUT GROUPS

Group 1	7 Mercury astronauts	April 1959
Group 2	9 test pilots	September 1962
Group 3	14 pilot astronauts	October 1963
Group 4	6 scientist astronauts	June 1965
Group 5	19 pilot astronauts	April 1966
Group 6	11 scientist astronauts	August 1967
Group 7	7 MOL pilots	August 1969
Group 8	15 pilot astronauts and 20 mission specialists	January 1978

Total selected: 108

Still active: 62 –

PILOTS
Group 1: Slayton. *Group 2* Young, STS 1 commander. *Group 3:* Bean, probable Spacelab 1 commander. *Group 5:* Brand, STS test flight commander; Engle, STS test flight commander; Lousma, STS test flight pilot; Mattingly; McCandless; Pogue; Weitz. *Group 7:* Bobko; Crippen, STS 1 pilot; Fullerton, STS test flight pilot; Hartsfield; Overmyer; Peterson; Truly, STS test flight pilot. *Group 8:* Brandenstein; Coats; Covey; Creighton; Gibson; Gregory, Griggs; Hauck; McBride; Nagel; Scobee; Shaw; Shriver; Walker; Williams.

MISSION SPECIALISTS
Group 4: Garriott, Spacelab 1; Gibson; Kerwin. *Group 5:* Lind. *Group 6:* Allen; Henize; Lenoir; Musgrave; Parker, Spacelab 1; Thornton. *Group 8:* Bluford; Buchli; Fabian; Fisher; Gardner; Hart; Hawley; Hoffman; Lucid; McNair; Mullane; Nelson; Onizuka; Resnik; Ride; Seddon; Stewart; Sullivan; Thagard; van Hoften.

7   FLIGHT OF THE SHUTTLE

Looking north towards Cape Canaveral, Florida, along the stretches of sand called Cocoa Beach, the star-filled sky is black except for a fan of bright light twelve miles away. The light comes from launch complex 39A, from where men were once sent to the Moon, and where the Space Shuttle sits vertically on the pad preparing for lift-off, illuminated by searchlights which colour the sky with yellowish streaks.

Although it is still hours before lift-off, the traffic around Cape Canaveral is unusually busy for four o'clock in the morning. All the roads leading to the Cape and the public viewing areas around it are jammed with cars and coaches. To the experienced observer who has seen it all before, the scene resembles a night during December 1972 when thousands flocked to witness the launch of Apollo 17, the last flight to the Moon.

One of the first flights of the Shuttle is about to begin. If this flight and those that follow it are successful, this scene will not be repeated because Shuttle launches will almost become as commonplace as flights of the Concorde. But, like the Concorde, the Shuttle will still attract some enthusiasts. After all, a lift-off is something to remember.

Only two astronauts are flying on the first few missions, but later, astronauts, mission specialists and payload scientists will all be flying together. The space-suited crew arrive at the launch pad in a special coach which has travelled a few miles from the Manned Spaceflight Operations Building. It is now two hours before launch.

Placing themselves in the Shuttle Orbiter cockpit, surrounded by switches, dials and controls, the reclining crew await blast-off whilst reading through the all-important pre-flight checklists. Outside this delta-winged dart, the launch pad is being cleared of all personnel. Only emergency rescue vehicles and crews, well protected from the launching blast, will remain in the vicinity of the

Opposite – lift-off   launch pad. Other workmen will retreat to the control centre, three

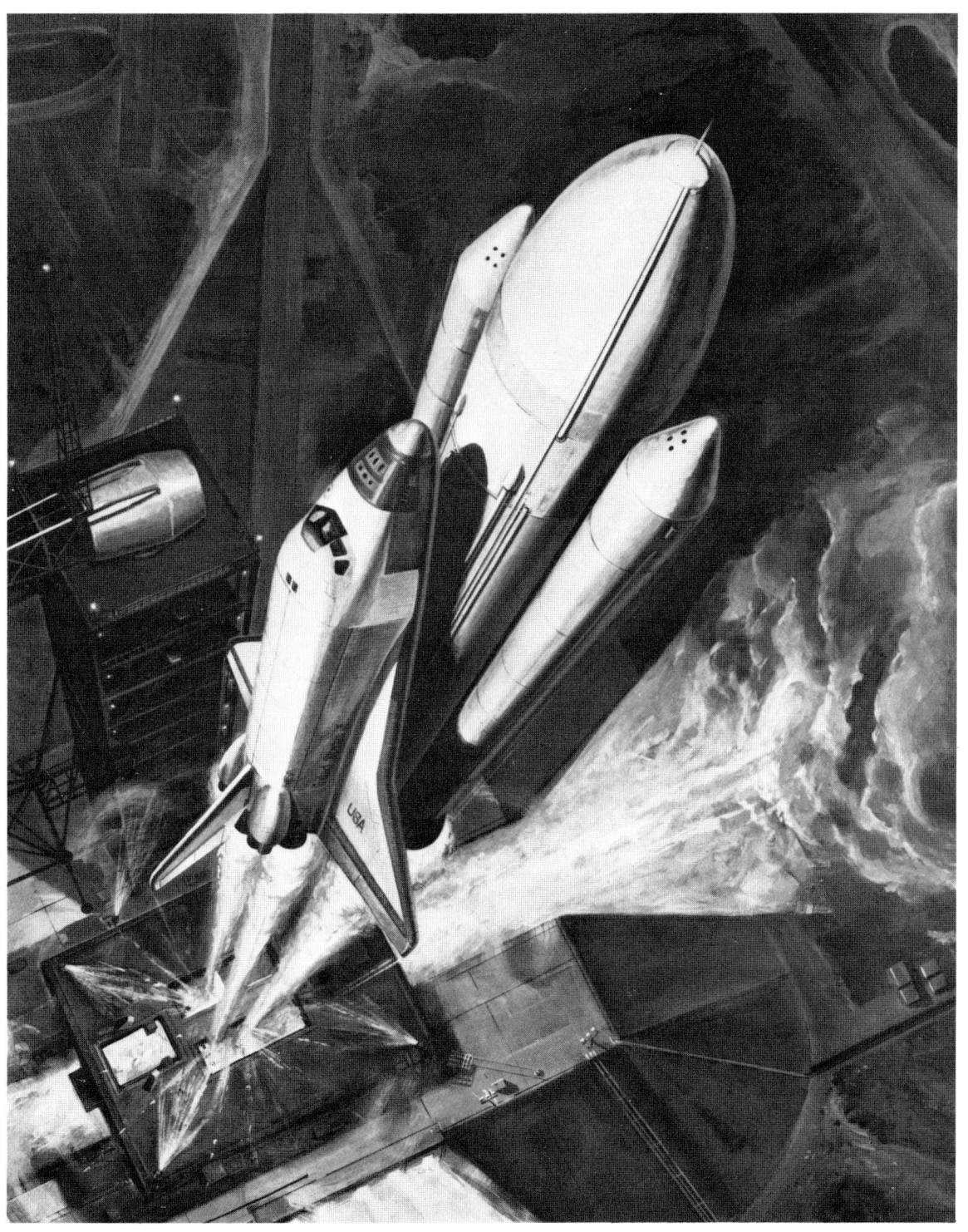

The Orbiter cockpit

miles away, to monitor the blast-off. The world's press are the nearest group of people to the launch pad, two and three quarter miles away. Further afield still are the general public.

The lift-off approaches. On the beaches of Cape Canaveral the Atlantic Ocean surges forth in monotonous waves. Seagulls hover. The wildlife in the almost tropical Cape is unaware that its peace is about to be shattered yet again by another rocket launch.

Suddenly flame belches out of the base of the Shuttle and smoke and steam gush out like a torrent of water from either side of the launch pad. The seagulls gyrate in demented arcs, the air is filled with the shrieks of wild birds which suddenly launch themselves in panic into the sky. While there is a great tremble and roar from the rocket, the sound has not yet reached the press site some miles away. Therefore the Shuttle seems to rise silently beneath a bright yellow and orange tongue of flame. It takes only three seconds to clear the launch tower and the Shuttle is 500 feet into the air before the noise finally reaches the press site, where newspaper, TV and radio reporters watch.

The ground trembles and the rocket exhaust makes a noise like a crackling and roaring bonfire. The crackles, like whip-lashes, are the shock waves pounding the air. The noise is terrific.

Soon, though, the noise is but a gentle murmur in the sky as the Shuttle disappears into a high blanket of cloud. For the press and viewing public the experience is all but over. For the astronauts and the Space Shuttle, the experience is beginning.

Beneath a thrust of 6.5 million pounds the Shuttle has arced over the Atlantic Ocean and is now upside down, with the external tank and solid rocket boosters on top of it. The five engines are consuming 11 tons of fuel every second as the strange-looking rocket combination races farther into space. It is two minutes into the flight. The acceleration forces press the astronauts into their seats. The forces measure 3G. This represents three times a spaceman's own weight. It is a little hard to breathe but to the astronauts, who on previous flights and during training have endured up to 12Gs, this is mere luxury. Indeed, it is really comfortable enough for an untrained passenger to fly.

At twenty-seven miles up, things begin to happen. The solid rocket boosters cease firing – their fuel is depleted. They are ejected and continue flying in a 'ballistic' arc before falling back towards the sea. At 22,000 feet drogue parachutes begin to slow them down, and at 6,000 feet main 'chutes open. The rockets splash down in the Atlantic Ocean, 184 miles down-range from the Cape, and are picked up by Naval recovery vessels which are to take them back to base for repair and reuse.

The Orbiter's three engines, fed with fuel from the external tank, take the vehicle, still upside down, to a height of over 100 miles. Eight minutes after lift-off, the engines shut down and the external tank is ejected. The Shuttle's orbital manoeuvring system bursts into life and the Shuttle reaches an orbital speed of 17,466 miles per hour. While the external tank is plummeting towards a fiery re-entry into the atmosphere and break-up over the Indian Ocean, the Shuttle's reaction control system's thrusters are turning the vehicle the right way up.

Boosters and external tank are jettisoned.

Once it is in orbit, the multiple missions of the Shuttle begin. These are described in the next chapter. While the Shuttle crews orbit the Earth on their missions, which will last up to 30 days, they live and work together in quite comfortable surroundings. They have a bedroom, a shower room, a toilet and a kitchen. One controlling factor is the weightlessness. The astronauts float around – unless they are restrained by harnesses.

Going to bed means the astronaut wrapping himself up in a cocoon-like sleeping bag so that he doesn't float away when he sleeps. The toilet is rather like one in an aircraft. The astronaut goes to the toilet by sitting on the seat and wrapping himself up in a restraining sheet. A vacuum pump aids flushing and avoids the problem of floating particles.

Weightlessness affects eating too. Although the astronaut can eat most of the foods he eats on Earth, the form in which they are produced is different.

Meals in space have come a long way since the toothpaste-tube food eaten by the early astronauts of the Mercury and Gemini missions. Research into the sort of food that can be eaten in weightlessness has resulted in the development of six types. These are called thermostabilised, intermediate moisture, rehydratable, irradiated, freeze-dried and natural. Thermostabilised food is canned food and food in tinfoil that can be heated and eaten with a spoon. Such food includes cheese spread, tuna fish and barbecue sauce. Intermediate moisture food includes dried apricots, peaches and breakfast cereal bars. Rehydratable foods are those reconstituted with water, such as scrambled egg and chicken and noodles and drinks, like coffee. Irradiated food is exposed to radiation to preserve it. Such food includes bread rolls and beefsteak. Freeze-dried foods such as strawberries, shrimps and bananas are eaten using the saliva in the mouth as the moistening agent. Nuts and biscuits are called 'natural' foods.

So, life aboard the Shuttle is by no means that unusual or different from the wardroom of a small ship. The only difference is weightlessness.

When the mission is ended, the Shuttle prepares for its re-entry. The orbital manoeuvring system engines are fired with the Shuttle facing nose down. This nudges the Orbiter out of orbit and into the thick layers of atmosphere where the fiery heat of re-entry begins. The orbit has been reduced to 76 miles altitude. The Shuttle

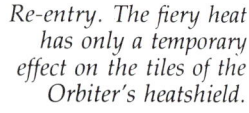

Re-entry. The fiery heat has only a temporary effect on the tiles of the Orbiter's heatshield.

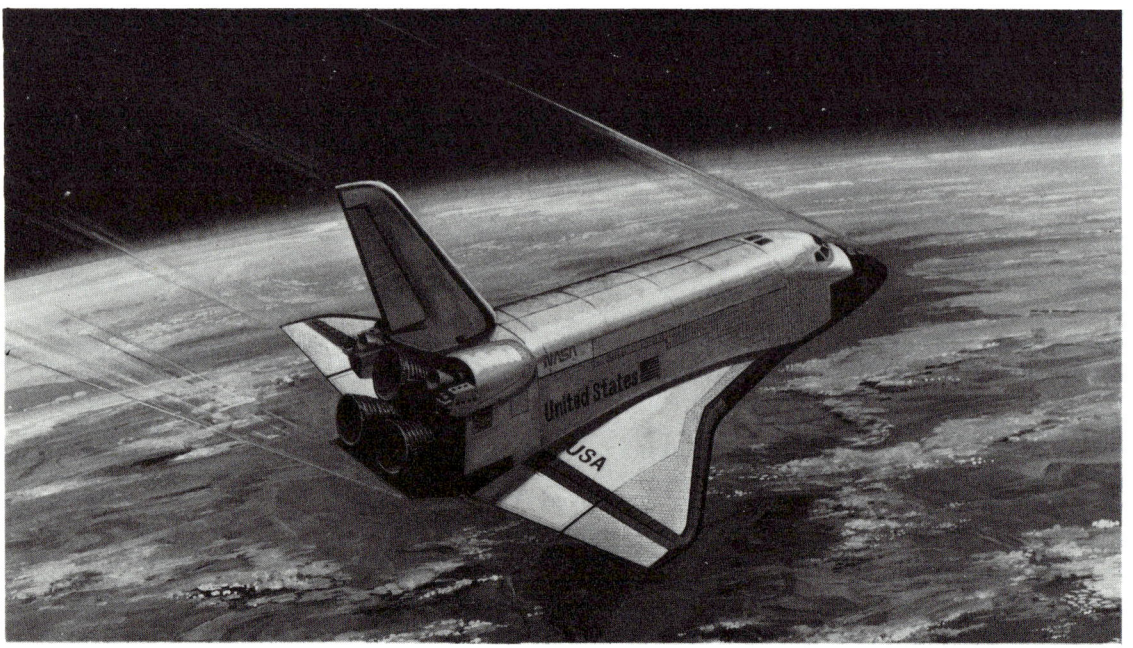

is still travelling at over 17,400 mph. Friction against the atmosphere acts like a brake, slowing this speed to about 5000 mph by the time the Orbiter has reached 150,000 feet.

Landing approach at Kennedy Space Center.

This re-entry is accompanied by beautiful and frightening audio-visual effects. At 400,000 feet the Shuttle first brushes the air with a whisper. The sky overhead is still black. Soon the craft heats up as it glides into the thicker layers of the air. The nose and leading edges of the wings and tail glow orange and other parts of the Orbiter red.

One mistake by the computer control or pilot and the Shuttle will move out of position, exposing the wrong, less protected, parts to the heat and the craft will become a blazing meteor. At 300,000

Touchdown at Edwards Air Force Base after the final ALT flight, October 1977.

feet the temperatures have climbed to 2700°F and the noise is a terrifying roar and crackle. The spaceplane is enveloped in a crimson cocoon, but inside the cockpit all is okay.

Eight minutes after the re-entry into the atmosphere, the craft is at 160,000 feet, and in order to slow down for a landing it begins to zig-zag across the sky. It is at this point that the spaceplane becomes an aircraft. Soon, the runway of Edwards Air Force Base is looming in front of the Orbiter as it automatically descends through 1700 feet at a nose-down angle of 24°, aided by a microwave landing system. At 184 mph it hits the runway and the on-board computer signals the braking system to operate. The Orbiter screams down the long runway, gradually coming to a stop. The mission has ended.

On later flights the landing will be made at Cape Canaveral. The sequence of launches will be such that launching at Canaveral will mean a landing there and a launching from the military base Vandenburg in California will end on a runway there.

The crew will leave the Orbiter and the spaceplane will be taken away to be refurbished for the next flight. After the early flights ending at Edwards Air Force Base the Orbiter is taken back to Cape Canaveral on the back of a giant Boeing 747 jumbo jet.

It will take 160 hours for the Shuttle to be made ready for another flight. By this time another Shuttle Orbiter could already be in space.

This is the flight sequence of the Shuttle. The missions that it will perform in space are described in the next chapters.

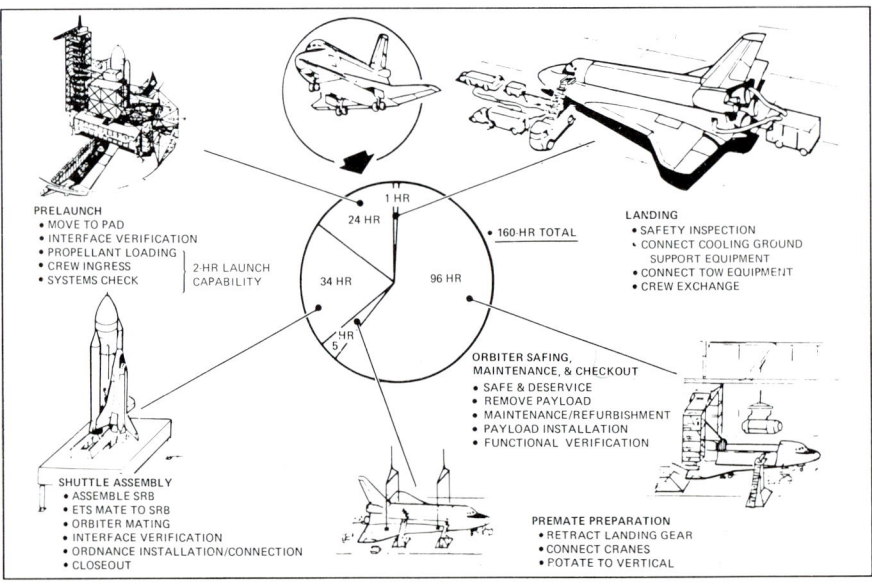

PRELAUNCH
• MOVE TO PAD
• INTERFACE VERIFICATION
• PROPELLANT LOADING
• CREW INGRESS
• SYSTEMS CHECK

2-HR LAUNCH CAPABILITY

1 HR
24 HR
• 160-HR TOTAL
34 HR
96 HR
5 HR

LANDING
• SAFETY INSPECTION
• CONNECT COOLING GROUND SUPPORT EQUIPMENT
• CONNECT TOW EQUIPMENT
• CREW EXCHANGE

ORBITER SAFING, MAINTENANCE, & CHECKOUT
• SAFE & DESERVICE
• REMOVE PAYLOAD
• MAINTENANCE/REFURBISHMENT
• PAYLOAD INSTALLATION
• FUNCTIONAL VERIFICATION

SHUTTLE ASSEMBLY
• ASSEMBLE SRB
• ETS MATE TO SRB
• ORBITER MATING
• INTERFACE VERIFICATION
• ORDNANCE INSTALLATION/CONNECTION
• CLOSEOUT

PREMATE PREPARATION
• RETRACT LANDING GEAR
• CONNECT CRANES
• POTATE TO VERTICAL

Ground turnaround time

THE FIRST MISSIONS

In addition to the fact that it is a reusable spacecraft and will reduce the cost of spaceflight, just how is the Space Shuttle going to revolutionise the future exploitation and exploration of space? By its very versatility.

It will be able to take a space station into orbit on one flight, take four spacecraft into orbit on another and 'launch' them from its payload bay into other orbits or towards the planets, and on a third retrieve a satellite, bringing it back to Earth for repair. A mini-space factory will be orbited on some missions, while on others the Shuttle will be used to take up into orbit parts of a large space station that will be assembled in space piece by piece. Other plans in store envisage its use for the building of a space power station and for use as a space 'garage' for in-orbit servicing and repairing of satellites.

By performing these different tasks more cheaply than using conventional expendable rockets, the Shuttle becomes an attractive commercial proposition to companies and organisations who wish to use it. Companies will call on the Shuttle to launch satellites for them or to perform other tasks in space.

Before doing these jobs and becoming a workable, commercial proposition to its customers, the Shuttle has to go through a rigorous flight test programme in space.

The Shuttle chosen for this job is No. 102, called Columbia. There will be five Shuttle Orbiters. The first, the Enterprise which was used for approach and landing tests in the atmosphere and subsequent pre-launch simulations and trials, may eventually be converted for space work. The third and fourth Orbiters to be built are called Atlantis and Discovery and the fifth is called Challenger.

Columbia is the Orbiter destined to fly the first test missions and the first operational flights.

Originally planned to take place in March 1979 the first test flight will not take place until about June 1980 and may be delayed still further. The Shuttle development programme has not been free of

The first Shuttle astronauts, photographed in March 1978: from the right – John Young, commander of STS 1, Robert Crippen, his pilot, Joe Engle, Dick Truly, Fred Haise, Jack Lousma, Vance Brand and Gordon Fullerton. Haise later resigned from the astronaut corps.

problems. The Space Shuttle Main Engine has failed many times during testing and obviously has to have many successful static tests behind her before she is entrusted with the maiden flight. Other problems have been encountered with the application of the thermal protection system and the preparation of computer software, or programmes, for the simulators used by astronauts to train for specific flights.

Six orbital flight tests were scheduled before the Shuttle was to become operational but because of development problems delaying the first launch, that number could be reduced to five or even four in order to meet the scheduled launch dates for many operational commercial flights which have tight deadlines.

The flight plans described in this chapter were prepared in July 1979 and are, of course, subject to change, particularly should the Shuttle programme be delayed still further. By the time the crew of the first flight eventually get into space they will have been in training for over two years, the longest ever specific flight training a crew has taken in the history of the US space programme.

The first flight, called STS 1, is piloted by John Young, the veteran astronaut on his fifth space flight, and new man, Robert Crippen. This will be the first time that men will have been launched on an untried rocket-spacecraft. Columbia will place itself in an orbit around the Earth about 190 miles up, with an inclination to the equator of 38°; that is the angle at which it crosses the equator. The flight will last 53 hours, during which the flight systems will be thoroughly tested. The crew will practise opening and closing the payload bay doors. A safe re-entry can be made with the doors slightly opened, but not fully. So if there is a problem with the automatic system the pilot will close the doors manually during EVA.

To ensure that the sun's rays fall evenly over the whole surface of the Shuttle, Young and Crippen will put the Orbiter into a 'barbecue' mode in which the Shuttle will slowly revolve with the aid of occasional firings of the reaction control system to induce a slow roll movement. On later flights, the barbecue mode will not be used; indeed quite the opposite, the Orbiter will be placed in one stable position in orbit for the operation of science packages. An earth resources camera, for example, would need to be pointed always at the Earth. The open doors of the Shuttle therefore would face the Earth's surface and the Shuttle would effectively be upside down for the duration of its flight.

The flight of STS 1 will end with Young and Crippen making de-orbit rehearsals before a re-entry and a manual approach and landing on the lake-bed runway at Edwards Air Force Base. The Shuttle will then be ferried back to Cape Canaveral on the back of a jumbo jet.

How does John Young feel about making his fifth spaceflight?

Spacelab 1 consists of a pressurised module and one pallet for experiment instruments which need direct exposure to space.

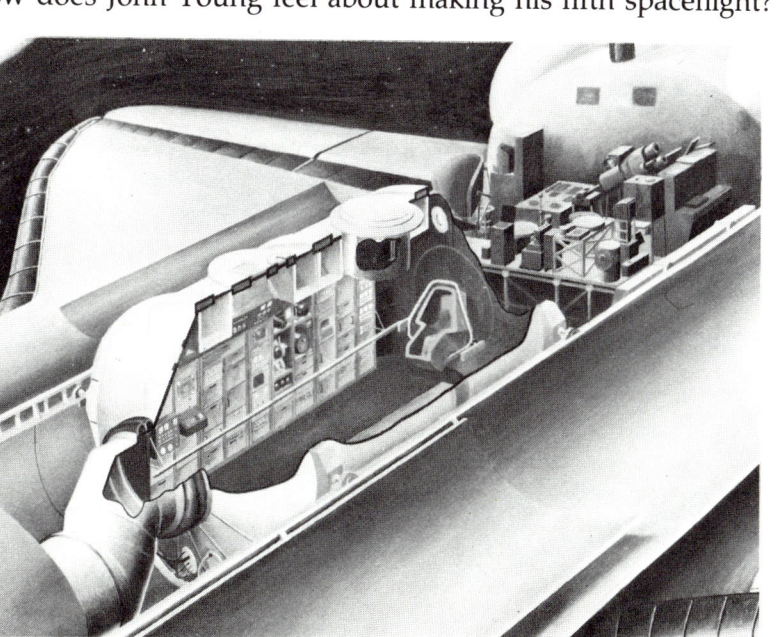

The 'launching' of a Tracking and Data Relay Satellite. The satellite is attached to its own rocket stage which will boost it into higher orbit.

He will be the first man to reach this milestone. He was asked the question at a press conference at the Houston space centre in March 1978. He said 'It's kind of difficult to get very excited about it this early in the game. This is an absolutely revolutionary flying machine. It's going to do things for spaceflight that will change the world. It's going to do things for aviation that will change aviation, I think in ways that even those of us that are involved in it can't imagine. So it's going to be a very, very exciting mission for all of us. There are no "bad" missions on spaceflights but comparing this one with going to the Moon is like comparing apples and oranges and I don't think you can do that fairly. But it's going to be very, very interesting to work on and very interesting to participate in.'

Should the first flight of the Shuttle be put further behind schedule to such an extent that it places pressure on later test flights which have to be completed in order to meet payload launching deadlines, the maiden mission could well be a ballistic, 'up and down' flight primarily to test the launch system and the thermal protection tiles.

The second STS test flight four months later will further develop the system. If STS 1 is a success, this flight will be piloted by Engle and Truly. STS 2 will stay in orbit for up to five days with the payload doors open during the duration of the orbital stay. Its mission complete, STS 2, like its predecessor, will land on the dry lake-bed runway of Edwards Air Force base.

During the third STS flight the manipulator arm may be tested. On later flights the arm will be used to deploy satellites in orbit by lifting them out of the payload bay and releasing them in space. The arm will also be used on other missions to retrieve satellites and gather them into the payload bay. During STS 3 the arm will go through the simulated movements of deploying a dummy satellite.

The manipulator is called the Remote Manipulator System, or RMS. It is 50 feet long. Its 'shoulder' joint is situated about seven feet behind the main cockpit and will be able to move up and down and from side to side, these movements being called pitch and yaw. The 'elbow' unit that connects the two boom sections of the arm will be able to pitch, while its 'wrist' will be able not only to pitch and yaw but to roll as well, turning around on its axis to face in any direction.

Plans for later test flights are not definite and will depend to a great extent on the success of the previous flight. One of these later missions will attempt a fully automatic landing at Edwards Air Force Base. Flight four will probably see the first landing at Cape Canaveral,

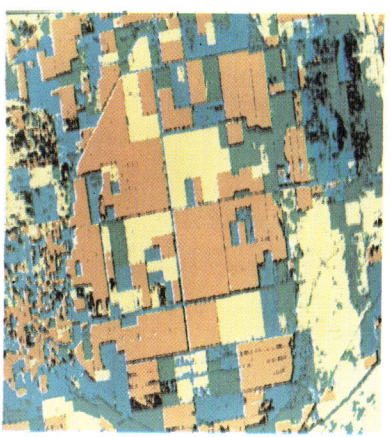

Landsat view of cultivated fields in the San Joaquin Valley, California, (left) provides the base data for the crop map (below) which shows red for cotton, yellow for safflower, green for wheat stubble and blue for fallow ground.

unless of course the STS 1 mission is a ballistic flight which will end there as a matter of course. Orbital inclinations of these missions will vary. Inclinations to the equator of 57° and 28° will be tried. It is quite possible also that more than two crewmen will fly a later test flight, possibly the fifth should there be one, and that a spacewalking attempt by an astronaut wearing the new Shuttle spacesuit and a manoeuvring unit will be made.

During the STS test missions, and indeed any Shuttle flight, there is of course the possibility of a failure. On the early STS test flights the crews will have ejection seats for emergency evacuation during the most serious of launch failures, the exploding rocket. However, it is hoped that the Shuttle engines and solid rocket boosters provide a reliable enough system to avoid such disastrous events. Other abort eventualities have been identified and plans to cater for them introduced.

There are three abort situations – Return to Launch Site (RTLS), Abort Once Around (AOA), and Abort to Orbit (ATO).

RTLS occurs should one of the Orbiter's main engines fail early in the flight. The Shuttle combination will fly to 58 miles altitude before turning back, jettisoning the external tank and landing on the runway at the launch site 20 minutes after lift-off.

AOA caters for problems occurring during the second half of the ascent into orbit. Should an engine failure occur here, the Orbiter is placed on a path that just falls short of orbital speed, which means that the craft flies in a 'ballistic' flight path, or trajectory, once around the Earth – effectively one orbit – before landing back at the launch site.

ATO is selected in the event of problems that do not call for the immediate return to Earth, such as a computer or fuel cell failure. In this case the Shuttle will achieve orbit and then will be brought back to one of fifteen contingency landing sites around the world.

These test flights may, time and test mission schedules permitting, carry science experiments in the payload bay. If they are not carried on these flights they will be flown on later operational flights. These experiments are as follows.

Inside the payload bay will be a pallet containing the IECM or Induced Environment Contamination Monitor, which is being flown on all STS orbital test flights.

The importance of the IECM is that it will be used to find out whether the operation of the Shuttle Orbiter will affect the results of the experimentation it carries. Will the venting of the gases and fuel during manoeuvres affect the monitors of science experiments? This is what the IECM will find out.

On some flights the Shuttle Orbiter will fly upside down exposing to Earth a package of earth resources experiments in a pallet. This package will make investigations into 'all weather surface observation'.

Previously, many aircraft and satellites have been used to take photographs very successfully of the Earth to detect various resources, like oil and minerals, and such things as soil conditions and crop yields. These photos have been taken in two ways, through filters of the infra-red and visible spectrums. The visible spectrum is how we see things, but we do not see infra-red. Both these methods are fine provided there is no cloud cover. This Shuttle experiment will use a microwave radar system that will be able to see the surface through cloud.

Another experiment will be used to detect pollution in the upper atmosphere. Also, infra-red photos will be taken to detect areas on the Earth rich in different types of minerals, oil and gas. An 'Ocean Colour Experiment' will try to identify areas of the oceans that are rich in concentrations of a sea chemical called chlorophyll, an indication of the presence of small sea organisms called plankton and algae, by detecting changes in the colour of the

Landsat D Earth Resources spacecraft launched from the Shuttle.

sea. The presence of plankton and algae would indicate that the area was rich in fish life and that this would obviously be a good place in which to fish.

A final experiment will look closely at the connection between the convection currents in clouds and the outbreak of lightning and thunder, with a view to learning more about this meteorological phenomenon.

The Shuttle Orbiter will be equipped with the 'Long Duration Exposure Facility' or LDEF for short. The LDEF will be li''ed out of the payload bay by the manipulator arm and will be left in orbit for up to a year, after which it will be retrieved by another Shuttle.

Spacewalking astronauts working on a satellite payload in the Shuttle Orbiter payload bay.

The Long Duration Exposure Facility (LDEF) in the payload bay of the Shuttle Orbiter. A variety of passive experiments can be mounted on LDEF so that the effects of exposing them to space conditions can later be assessed.

The LDEF is an unmanned, reusable free flying facility on which many different technical and scientific experiments can be mounted on special trays. It will carry nearly fifty science experiments.

The LDEF is designed to expose materials to space conditions so that they can be analysed when they return to Earth. Other experiment packages will detect and measure radiation in space coming from the stars and the sun. One such experiment is called the 'Interstellar Gas Experiment'. This was designed by scientist-astronaut Don Lind. The experiment will 'analyse the interstellar noble gas atoms that penetrate the heliosphere'.

The structure of gas radiation from stars that reaches the region between the sun and the Earth varies considerably. The LDEF experiment as it orbits the Earth, as the Earth itself orbits the sun, will therefore sample the gas in different areas of space. In this way it may be possible to map the 'wind' that carries the radiation, called the interstellar wind, and see how it interacts with radiation coming out of the sun. All these things may seem remote when considering their connection with life on Earth, but interstellar gas, solar wind and radiation in space all have an effect on the Earth, its atmosphere and its weather.

Five materials-processing experiments will be packaged in a Materials Experiment Assembly called the MEA. Weightlessness provides an ideal environment in which to manufacture some materials and the MEA will give scientists an interim opportunity to conduct investigations into the technology before such experiments are carried out on Spacelab missions.

If all goes according to plan after no more than six test flights the operational era of the Space Transportation System will open.

One of the major jobs of the Shuttle will be the placing or deployment of satellites in orbit, the launching of satellites into deeper orbits and the launching of space probes. This will take place from the payload bay. The Shuttle's orbit is low, but most satellites will need to be placed in high, geostationary orbits – ones in which the speed of the satellite matches that of the speed of the rotation of the earth. These orbits are also called synchronous and in them the satellite appears stationary in the sky. Such an orbit is particularly useful for communications and meteorological or weather satellites, because they are continually over the same area of the Earth.

In order to send these satellites into synchronous orbits and send space probes towards the planets, the Shuttle's payloads will be equipped with special rockets called stages, which will be in the payload bay and to which the satellite or probe will already be attached. These stages are called SSUS and IUS.

The SSUS is a 'Spinning Solid Upper Stage' rocket and two types, the SSUS-D and SSUS-A, have been built.

The SSUS-D will carry single satellite payloads weighing between 2000 and 2400 pounds. The SSUS-A will be able to carry payloads from 4000 to 4400 pounds. These two stages are designed in conjunction with the Shuttle, to replace the existing expendable Thor Delta and Atlas Centaur satellite launchers. Each SSUS is attached to a 'spin-table' in the Shuttle's payload bay. Up to four SSUS-D units and two SSUS-A units can be carried on a single flight, each with separate payloads.

Launching a satellite with an SSUS into a synchronous orbit will involve launching the Shuttle into a 160-mile orbit with, say, an inclination to the equator of 28.5°. The SSUS, plus its satellite payload, will be automatically positioned upright on its spin-table to point out of the open Shuttle payload bay. The stage will then be spun at between 65 and 100 revolutions per minute and released from the Orbiter. This effectively stabilises the rocket stage.

Once a safe distance away from the Shuttle, the SSUS engine will ignite at the moment that it crosses over the equator. This will cause not only an increase in orbital height but also a plane change. The satellite will begin to orbit the Earth around the equator.

The SSUS will take the payload into a 160 mile by 19,323 mile 'geostationary transfer orbit', after which the satellite will separate from the SSUS and another rocket motor on the satellite itself, called an apogee motor, will be used to circularise the orbit at a height of 22,000 miles. This is a synchronous or geostationary orbit.

The IUS, or Inertial Upper Stage, has been developed to launch much heavier military satellites weighing 5000 pounds into geostationary orbits. About 96% of all payloads carried by the IUS will be military satellites. The remainder will be used to launch NASA probes to the planets.

There will be four different types of IUS: a military/NASA two-stage rocket, a military twin-stage, a NASA twin-stage and a NASA three-stage rocket.

The basic two-stage vehicle is 16.4 feet long and consists of a bottom stage, with 21,400 pounds of solid propellant delivering a thrust of 42,600 pounds, and a forward stage, containing 6000 pounds of the same propellant with a thrust of 17,000 pounds. Military, Department of Defense IUS versions have two stages together called a twin-stage. They each have motors with 42,600 pounds thrust. The NASA twin-stage is similar. The NASA three-stage consists of the basic twin-stage IUS with a 17,430-pound thrust upper stage. All IUS types are 7.6 feet in diameter widening at the bottom to 9.5 feet.

The IUS can hurl a satellite weighing 5000 pounds into geostationary orbit, a probe of 11,000 pounds to the inner planets of Mercury, Venus or Mars, and a 3300 pounds payload to Jupiter or to Saturn.

A further development in this technology is the Space Tug or TRS, the Teleoperator Retrieval System. This will be released from the Shuttle to make rendezvous with another satellite. It will secure itself to the satellite and return it to the Shuttle, all by remote control with the aid of on-board TV cameras and a monitor in the Shuttle cockpit. The TRS will also be provided with propulsion units to give it a boosting capability.

The TRS is a box-like structure, four feet by four feet by five feet, with three sets of attitude control thrusters at each corner. Twenty-four thrusters each with a thrust of 10 pounds will give TRS three axis and forward and backward manoeuvring capability. The central part of the TRS or 'cone' houses guidance, navigation and control systems, a communications and data management system and the propellant tank. A docking system is mounted on the forward end of the cone, together with two TV cameras. The TRS is equipped with strap-on propulsion systems or kits. Each is three feet in diameter and five feet long and carries 1500 lbs of hydrazine propellant and eight rocket engines of 25 pounds thrust each, giving a total thrust of 200 pounds. The TRS can carry a total of four kits. It will be controlled with the aid of hand controls in the Shuttle cockpit, the pilot using a TV monitor showing pictures fed from the TRS cameras.

Another important piece of Shuttle equipment is the TDRSS satellite which itself will be launched by the Shuttle. TDRSS stands for Tracking and Data Relay Satellite System. A number of these satellites will eventually be launched into synchronous orbits to cater for the flood of data and communications that is going to result from the exploitation of space by the Shuttle.

A new communications network, capable of relaying larger volumes of information than existing facilities, will be established by a network of TDRSS satellites, the first of four of which will be sent into orbit by an SSUS stage from an early Shuttle flight.

Two TDRSS satellites, one placed over the Atlantic at 41°W and one over the Pacific at 171°W, will relay communications from the Shuttle at any point in its orbit to a single ground station at Roswell,

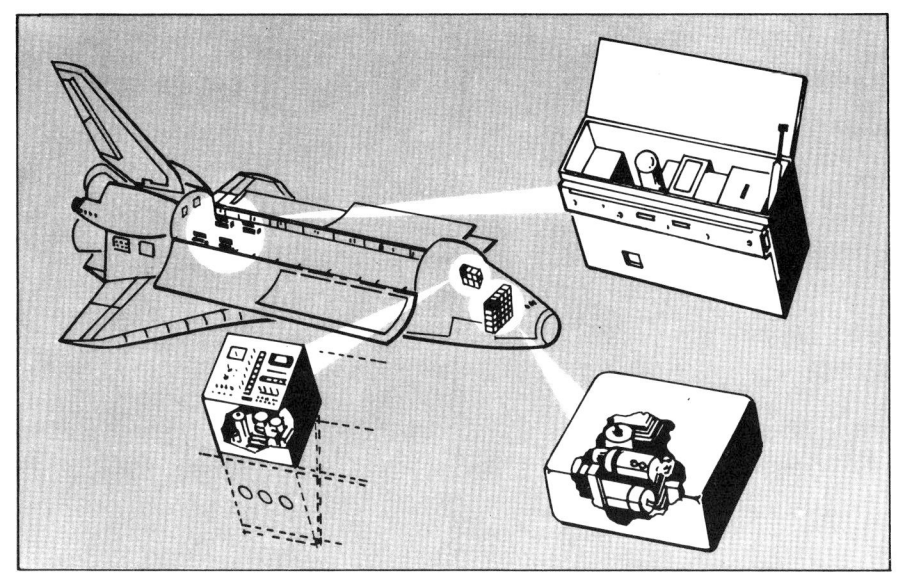

Where 'get-away-specials' are placed in the Shuttle Orbiter.

New Mexico, for onward transmission. The American telecommunications company, Western Union, is providing the satellites and NASA will lease them as and when required.

On the Shuttle flight that launches the first TDRSS another satellite will be launched. Called SBS it is the first in a series of satellites privately funded by companies for business communications.

By selling its services not only as a satellite launcher but as a reusable, recoverable space facility for experimenters, the Shuttle will be entirely funded from commercial sources – not public, taxpayers' money.

And the customer will save. It costs £12 million to have a satellite launched by an Atlas Centaur rocket. The Shuttle costs £10 million and on one flight can carry four such satellites, so the cost can be split four ways. A Thor Delta rocket launch costs £7 million and the Shuttle can launch a similar payload for £4 million.

In addition, the payload bay and other areas of the Orbiter will be equipped with large numbers of private experiment packages. Areas in the payload bay to carry such experiments are being sold by NASA, and any university, company or individual which has the money can have an experiment package sent into space.

At the low end of the fare structure is the 'get-away-special' which permits an organisation or an individual to book equipment space on the Shuttle on a space-available basis for between £1500 and £5000.

What sort of payloads will fly on the 'get-away-specials'? At the time of writing, NASA has already signed up 157 customers from all over the world. Thirty-three of these are private individuals who want to test out new ideas in space, 24 are from high schools, colleges and universities whose students are to participate in the use of space, particularly weightlessness or zero g, for experimentation, and 99 are for industrial packages that involve such things as pharmaceutical research and materials processing.

Five 'get-away-specials' can be carried on each flight. One pharmaceutical company will be using its experiment package to study blood plasma in weightlessness. Another company is interested in the surface effects of glass or other substances melted in zero gravity

The Shuttle has been booked for up to 30 flights. In addition to the 'get-away-special' science packages, the schedule at present has the first operational Shuttle launching a communications test satellite, called Syncom and possibly carrying an earth resources camera. However the plan could change and we may see another payload on the first operational flight. Another early flight will send up the first of the vital TDRSS satellites together with a Satellite Business Systems craft. Other payloads for early missions include GOES satellites, standing for Geostationary Operational Environmental Satellite, Telesat, the first in a new series of Canadian communications satellites and the largest ever communications satellite, Intelsat 5. A military satellite called Real Ruby is scheduled for an early flight also. Real Ruby is designed to explore the possibility of detecting military aircraft from space. One flight will be used to retrieve the LDEF satellite and bring it back to Earth. Three Spacelab flights are planned in the early schedule, the first of which will carry the first Western European into orbit and the second of which will orbit an all American scientist crew.

Many of these payloads, Spacelab excepted, will have to be launched by expendable rockets to meet launch deadlines should the first Shuttle flight be delayed still further. One certain launch will be the despatch of the Galileo Jupiter orbiter spacecraft in January 1982. The flight has to take place then because there is a tight 'launch window' during which it is possible to take advantage of the relative position of the planets, Earth and Jupiter, to make such a flight possible. If the Shuttle schedule is delayed for a very long time then plans will be made to launch Galileo by a Titan Centaur rocket, which was used to launch the recent Voyager spacecraft to Jupiter and Saturn.

THE FUTURE OF THE SHUTTLE 9

By 1982 the Space Shuttle will really be into the swing of things. A total of 650 flights of the Shuttle are scheduled to take place up to 1991 and apart from the type of missions discussed in the last chapter it will be used for more ambitious and exacting tasks.

Flights will begin from Vandenburg Air Force Base, California, in 1983. Vandenburg is being used for two reasons. Firstly, it is military space base. Many Shuttle missions during the 1980s will be of a military nature. Secondly, launching from Vandenburg makes a polar orbit possible, because a launching in a southerly direction over the South Pole can be safely made without the rocket passing over land.

A polar orbit is one in which a satellite circles the Earth around each pole, intersecting the equator at ninety degrees. In a polar orbit, a satellite can cover the whole world during one day as the Earth rotates beneath it. This can be very advantageous for satellites or Shuttle-based payloads designed to carry out earth resources experiments. In addition, as these orbits regularly take satellites over Russia and China and other important strategic targets, they are useful for military purposes.

Indeed, of the 113 Department of Defense military payloads flown by the Shuttle during the 1980s to 1991, 49 will be flown from Vandenburg into polar orbit. NASA will also use Vandenburg for science launches and the military agencies will use Cape Canaveral for other military flights.

There are many types of military satellites. Perhaps the most important is the 'spy-in-the-sky'. This is a reconnaissance satellite designed specifically to take close-up photos of military targets and either transmit these photos to Earth or return the developed photos to the ground in a special re-entry capsule. Spy satellites are useful to the military because they can fly over enemy territory un-noticed and cannot be shot down like a spy plane. The Shuttle will be used to launch such spy satellites during military exercises. It will also be used as a spy-in-space base itself, its payload bay crammed with sophisticated cameras and electronic equipment operated by trained space spies.

Other types of military satellite to be launched by the Shuttle are navigation satellites. With the right equipment, a user beaming into a navigation satellite such as Navstar can be told exactly where he is to within a few yards longitude and latitude, what time it is and how far he is from a known target. You can imagine how useful Navstar is to ships and aircraft and even troops on the move.

Communications satellites used to keep military agencies, armies, fleets and troops in touch with each other will also be sent into space by the Shuttle. Such a satellite is DSCS, or Defense Satellite Communications System. Another is Fleet Satcom, which as the name implies, is used for naval communications.

Spies-in-space are not just restricted to photographic satellites either. Some are called 'ferrets'. These satellites intercept and decode radio and electronic signals being sent by the 'enemy'.

The Russians and Chinese, as well as the Americans, use military satellites but the advantage the Americans have is that the Shuttle will be able to launch more and heavier satellites cheaply.

Another ability of the Shuttle which will no doubt be put to good use is its rendezvous capability. It will be able to make contact with a military satellite and repair it in space, or perhaps bring it back home for repair. It could of course be used to 'capture' enemy satellites and render them inactive!

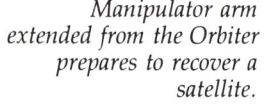

Manipulator arm extended from the Orbiter prepares to recover a satellite.

Some of the things that the military superpowers will be able to get up to in space are pretty frightening. Russia and America are already testing ways to destroy enemy satellites in orbit using laser beams and other methods. There is no reason therefore why the Shuttle could not be utilised to conduct such activities.

The military uses of outer space are regrettable but necessary. A balance of power can be maintained if each country can keep track of the other's development. For example, America knows how many rocket bases and rockets Russia has and vice versa. Both countries realise that space is being used for military purposes and both mean to continue. The Shuttle will be an important element in the development of military uses in space.

The majority of the Shuttle's missions will be used for the peaceful exploration and use of space. As we have seen, it will be used to send space probes out on their way to the planets. A prime example of this is the Galileo Jupiter probe being flown in 1982. Other probes will include a comet sample mission which will try to send a probe towards and on a 'collision' course with a comet. A

Infra-red photograph of a comet shows its different components.

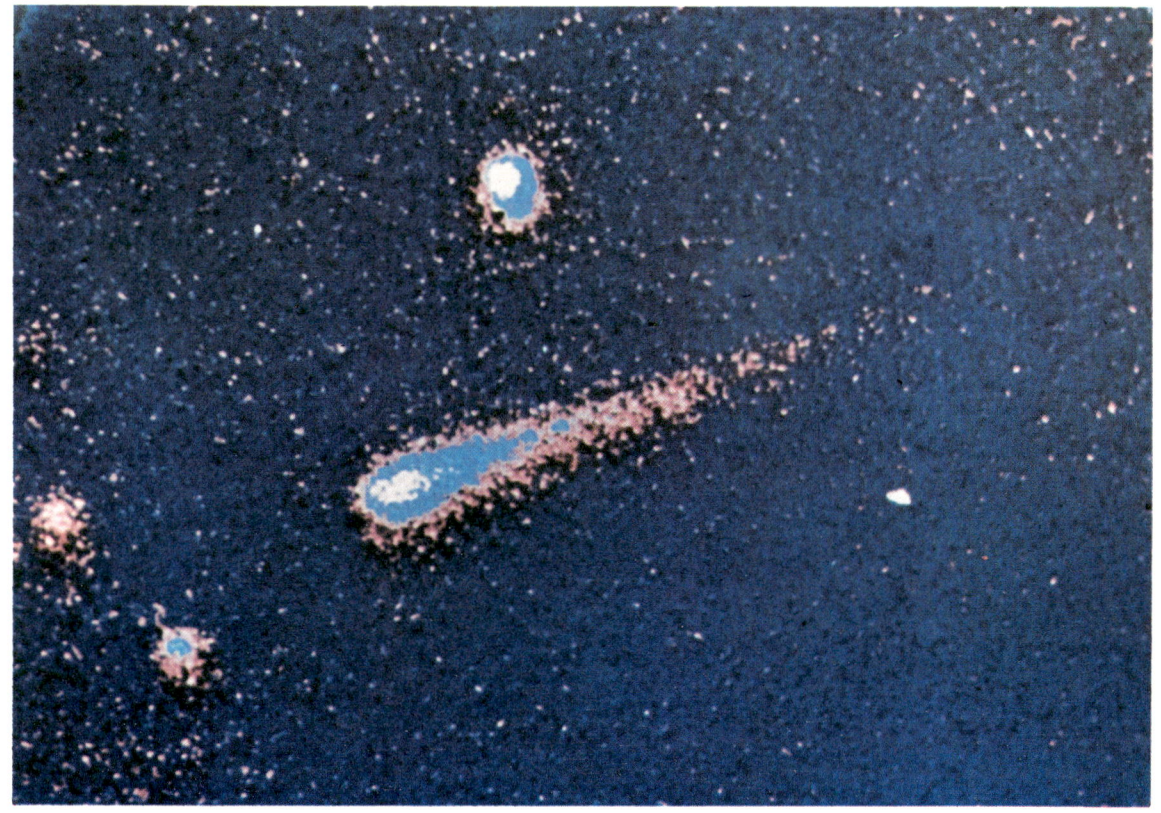

comet is a mass of gas, dust and ice particles which orbit the sun. When they approach the sun, they are illuminated in the sky. The probe will fly through the material making up the comet and will be able to analyse it as well as send back photos from close up of one of these strange celestial bodies.

Another probe envisaged is a Mars sample return mission which will land on Mars, pick up some Martian rock and soil and return it to Earth for analysis. The Shuttle would not only be used as a 'launch pad' in orbit to send the probe on its way but would also 'catch' it on the way back and return to Earth. A Martian aeroplane is another possible Shuttle payload. This will assemble itself into a propeller-driven aircraft as it enters the Martian atmosphere and will fly over the surface taking close-up pictures on the way.

In the later 1980s the Shuttle will probably be used to take up a space station in pieces into orbit flight-by-flight and assemble it like a Meccano set using its manipulator arm, teleoperator system and men walking in space. Such a space system envisaged is the space power station which will consist of enormous wings containing solar cells. These will collect the sun's rays and will convert the energy into electricity. Many satellites are powered in this way. This electrical energy will then be beamed down into a standard electric power station.

A solar power station will be built during the flights of the Shuttle to beam electricity to Earth. (Inset) A huge solar array wing, consisting of solar cells which will convert the sun's energy into electricity, tested in a Shuttle experiment.

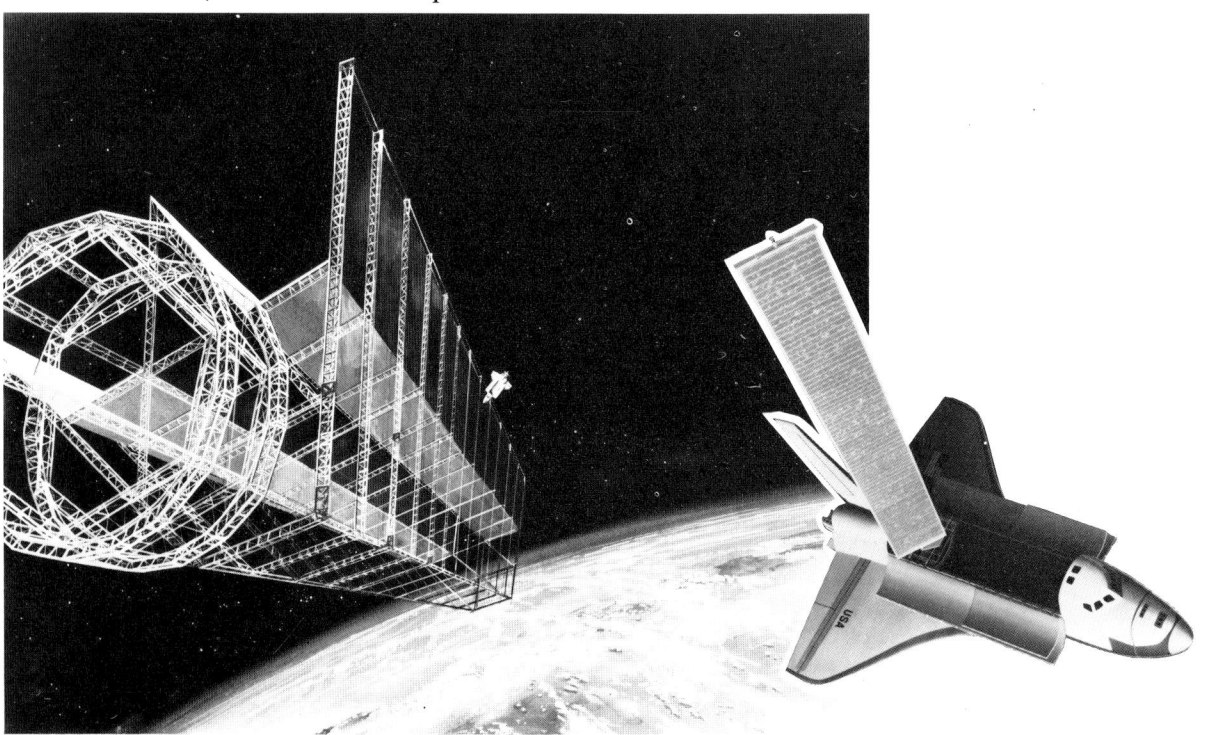

A space station being built around a Shuttle external tank.

Assembly of a large space structure, piece by piece, from the Shuttle.

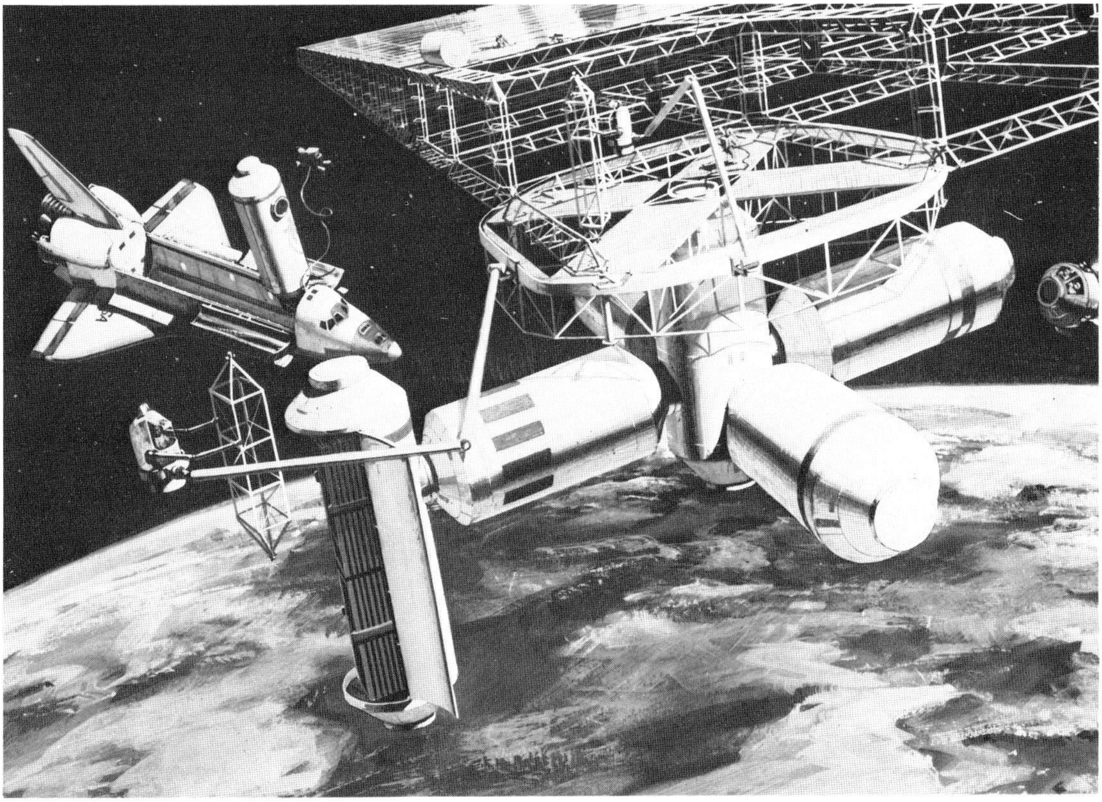

Later space stations will be built to continue many of the tasks which the Shuttle will be performing on a smaller scale during the early eighties. The Shuttle will use space with a view to improving life on Earth and our understanding of it. Many satellites will be launched and many experiments will be performed from Spacelab and the instrument-packed Shuttle payload bay which will prove the importance of space to mankind.

The Shuttle will help improve food production, our knowledge of natural resources, the environment and the weather. It will improve communications, conduct space manufacturing and processing tests and carry out basic research into astronomy. Here are some examples of how it will be used in these areas.

Earth resources spacecraft launched from the Shuttle, experiments carried out from its payload bay or by Spacelab can take photographs of areas of the Earth to enable crop inventories or surveys to be made. Photos already taken through different filters by satellites such as Landsat have demonstrated the potential of making crop surveys from space which can increase accuracy and save time. Photographs can enable the forecasting of volumes of coming harvests and contribute to decisions on new plantings to meet demand. Just one photograph of Imperial Valley in California taken from space made possible the inventory of 458,000 acres in 40 hours. Twenty-five crops were identified in over 8000 fields.

As the population of the world grows, it is becoming increasingly important to produce crops best suited to each part of the Earth's surface. Satellite photography has shown that good agricultural land is frequently lost through unplanned and unguided urban growth, and can be used to ensure that agricultural land is better utilized.

Images from space provide early warning of crop-destroying weeds, insects and diseases. For example, the Dudain melon is a weed that smothers crops. Losses caused by the infestation of this weed to asparagus growers in the US alone cost about £1½ million a year. In infra-red photos of asparagus fields the vegetable showed up purple and the melon crimson.

A weather satellite using infra-red imagery can locate areas of 'upwelling' in the areas of the coast. For example, strong winds from the north and north-west blow along California's coast, and the coastal surface water is moved offshore and replaced through upwelling. In upwelling areas, the colder nutrient-rich ocean bottom water rises to the surface of the ocean where huge blooms of plankton are formed. Plankton is the primary food for marine

LANDSAT PREDICTS WHEAT PRODUCTION

23 OCT 73   24 FEB 74   27 MAY 74   02 JULY 74

life. This attracts bait fish, which attract tuna and salmon.

One satellite passes over this coastal area twice daily, relaying the upwelling information to Earth where it is transferred to navigation charts that are furnished to fishermen.

Landsat pictures enabling scientists to monitor and predict wheat production.

Space photos provide rapid regional evaluation of flood hazards by quickly surveying areas of land susceptible to flooding. This can be done more accurately than standard engineering and hydraulic methods. Mapping flood susceptibility areas and flood hazard zones has obvious social and economic benefits.

Melting snows and heavy rains together can flood valuable farmland. The Mississippi River for example has, at various times, inundated many acres of fertile river valley land. Space photographs have revealed the extent of the flooding and areas most severely affected. This information was available in hours from satellites; it would have taken days to collect it by aircraft and weeks by surface inspection.

Geological mapping is necessary in the search for underground water, oil, minerals, and earthquake faults. There is a general misconception that the geology of the entire United States has been mapped in detail. Many parts have been, but there are vast regions for which only generalized maps have been prepared. Earth-orbital photography provides surveys of large areas and remote areas that would require a tremendous amount of time done by conventional means; in some cases it would be extremely difficult or even impossible to make the survey on the ground.

One satellite in orbit takes a picture of the Earth every 25 seconds. Each of those pictures covers an area 115 × 115 miles. In comparison, it would take thousands of aerial pictures to cover a 115-square-mile area and its costs would be more than £50,000. At this rate it would require millions of pounds to cover the world with aeroplanes. The satellite sends back the equivalent of a '£50,000 picture' every 25 seconds.

These pictures are studied by the geologists for the subtle signs in the search of resources. The images from space bring out items never known before and are being used as a new tool by the geologist and mineralogist in looking for mineral, petroleum, coal and oil deposits.

A United States geological survey found from photographs taken by astronauts on the Skylab space station that potential mineral deposits could provide the source of electric power the potential generator capability of which is equivalent to 140 large nuclear power plants or 140 Hoover Dams.

In Bolivia in 1972, the city of Santa Cruz printed maps of its surrounding area which were compiled from many aerial photographs taken between 1950 and 1969 and which involved hundreds of working hours to prepare. In 1974 a revision of these maps was made from two photographs taken in June 1973 from a satellite and required only 24 working hours to prepare.

Space photographs are also useful in the study of forestry. An American paper company is using space photos to survey its 1.6 million acres of forests in Alabama, Florida, Georgia, Louisiana and Mississippi.

This survey has already demonstrated the technical and economic effectiveness of space data in monitoring timber resources for indentification of trees. The data is also used in estimating timber volume and productivity and implementing techniques to detect changes in the health and growth of the forests.

One satellite observed a 60,000-acre commercial forest tract in the Southern Pines region of North Carolina and, through the use of computer analysis, distinguished accurately between stands of hardwood and pine. In some instances, these broad forest categories can be subdivided even further, yielding information useful in the routine management of the forest.

This provides an updated timber inventory, including estimates of board feet of soft and hardwood approaching market conditions. By combining this information with other records on a continuing basis, forest managers can ascertain growth rate and quality of forest stands as well as identify unauthorised cutting.

Remote sensing by space photography is also a unique tool for determining the variability of soils and terrain characteristics. These influence the amount of water retained in the soil and thus determine the soil moisture over large areas.

Photographs from space can aid pollution control too. For example, space-produced images can track and locate actual sources of air pollution while ground monitors cannot necessarily pinpoint such sources. Air pollution today is being observed as to its effects on weather conditions.

Air pollution over the Great Lakes in North America has been observed to modify weather. In the Chicago-Gary area, smoke plumes from steel mills and power plants flow out over Lake Michigan and feed directly into cumulus clouds over the lake. The clouds forming out of the plumes begin noticeably closer to the Illinois-Indiana shore and become denser and more well-developed as they approach the Michigan shore than do the clouds forming outside the direct lines of the smoke plumes. Because snow and rain form round particles, the clouds in the direct line of the plumes are more likely to produce precipitation than the other clouds. This is a clearly observable example of how human activities can change the weather.

A scientific study strongly suggests that a better understanding of global climate would help to solve two of the Earth's most pressing problems: food production and the possibility that the atmosphere might be sufficiently changed by pollutants to induce a worldwide change in the weather.

A scientific report in the US estimates that a 1° cooling of the Earth's average temperature per year would mean a drastic loss in wheat and rice production, in fish catch, and a loss in timber and fibre output around the world. In addition, the 1° drop would cause an increase in the annual electrical energy demand and a rise in health costs.

Meteorological observations from space.

Satellites can be used to monitor the Earth's climate in order to increase our knowledge and understanding of how it works.

For example, the GOES satellites launched by the Space Shuttle are typical of these kinds of spacecraft. GOES satellites are in synchronous orbit and two satellites are maintained in operational status; one at about 135°W longitude observing North America and the Pacific Ocean to the west of Hawaii, and the other at about 75°W observing both North and South America and the Atlantic Ocean and parts of the African west coast. The GOES system provides visual and infra-red pictures.

Visual and infra-red imagery is used to study cloud cover, wind, fog distribution, storm circulation, ocean currents, and snow melt, and to help in severe storm tracking, freeze forecasting, inland water ice evaluation, ship routing, and upwelling location. Imagery and digital read-outs provide wind speed and direction data at various heights for weather analysis and cloud height determination.

The GOES satellites also transmit weather charts and satellite information to weather offices throughout the Western Hemisphere for preparation of local and area weather forecasts. The satellites collect more than 10,000 observations every six hours. The spacecraft also provide data for measuring solar activity, solar wind intensity – that is radiation from the sun – and the strength and direction of Earth's magnetic field. This is used to predict the solar effect on communications and electric power generation and for radiation warning for manned spaceflights and for high-altitude aircraft.

Tropical storm photographed from space.

X-ray photograph of the solar corona.

Satellites such as Seasat study the oceans. Recent collisions of oil-carrying supertankers with shallow obstructions highlight the need for updating of world navigation charts, especially in well travelled areas. These collisions are often the result of unreliable information on the location of obstacles and their depth. Remote sensing from space is a means of providing this information for new navigation charts.

Using a NOAA satellite in a study, a researcher has developed a method that could give aeroplane pilots up to 12 minutes warning of clear-air turbulence ahead. The satellite uses an infra-red radiometer, which measures water vapour by the radiation it emits to predict turbulence with a reliability of 81 per cent. Drastic changes in the amount of water vapour are often followed within a few minutes by turbulence.

Communication from space using satellites has proved one of the biggest advances in technology. Communications satellites provide the link for global transmission of voice, television, or high-speed data. More than a billion people can witness an event as it happens by television. Over 100 countries and territories on six continents use communications satellites. It is possible today to reach nearly 250 countries and territories from almost any telephone in America.

Twenty nations can be direct-dialled without operator assistance. From 1965 to 1974 transoceanic phone calls grew from 3,000,000 a year to more than 50,000,000; they are expected to increase to 200,000,000 by 1980.

Such communications satellites are Intelsat 5, Westar, RCA Satcom and Marisat, a satellite designed specifically for maritime communications.

The Space Shuttle will allow new research into space processing. In the processing of metals, minerals, or other fluids at high temperatures, the 'one-g' gravity on Earth prevents uniform mixtures from being achieved (because of sedimentation of the heavier materials).

The result of this is that electrical, optical and mechanical properties of the processed materials are not as perfect as they could be. In the weightlessness environment, gravitational effects are eliminated and dramatic improvements are achieved.

This is especially important to the electronics industry as it would significantly improve the electrical properties of semi-conductor materials and the growing of large, 'perfect' crystals.

Crystals are used in applications such as computer memories, communications, lasers, surface acoustics and ultrasonics. Glass crystals not obtainable in conventional glasses can be obtained in zero-g for advanced optical systems and laser applications.

Growing crystals in space.

High gravity metals and semi-conductors such as tungsten are desirable for X-ray tubes and beryllium is needed for neutron spectrometers. These materials are readily contaminated by their containers in Earth's gravity. Working in zero-g would therefore be advantageous.

Metallic structures, formed of very high temperature materials having unique properties, are produced by mixing the components together and heating them to a temperature high enough to fuse them but not to melt and intermix them. This process, called sintering, is used to produce bearings and filters, abrasive tools, electric lamp filaments, motors, dynamo brushes and a variety of soft and hard magnetic materials. In Earth's gravity, the porous structures tend to collapse under the gravitational stresses during the sintering process.

So, clearly, new and better products can be anticipated from space processing. In metallurgy, examples are magnets, catalysts, superconductors, alloys, lubricants, turbine blades, thermoelectrics, metal fibres, foam metals, fibre-reinforced metals, and high purity refractory materials. In glass crystals, examples include large silicon crystals, silicon ribbon, fibre optics, film memories, integrated circuit chips, space glass, semi-conductors, and semi-conducting glasses and solar cells.

Other research by the Space Shuttle will be made into astronomy. In addition to sending spacecraft to the planets, the Shuttle will launch a giant Space Telescope and carry out research from its payload bay into some of the mysteries of the universe – pulsars, quasars, exploding galaxies, and black holes in space.

Pulsars and neutron stars were discovered in 1967. Pulsars are stars which emit radio signals in extremely precise pulses. Evidence now suggests that pulsars may be fast-spinning compact stars comprising of densely packed neutrons believed to form when a large star burns up much of its fuel and collapses. They are so closely packed that a spoonful of material from the centre of a star 10 miles in diameter would weigh a billion tons.

Black holes are believed to be final stages in the collapse of a dying star. The star's material is so densely packed – even more so than a neutron star – and its gravitational force so great that even light waves are unable to escape from the surface.

Quasars are estimated to be less than 10 light years in diameter, compared to the 100,000 light-year diameter of a typical galaxy of 100 billion stars, yet quasars pour out 100 times more energy. They are the most powerful emitters of energy known. How this energy is generated is a mystery. No known physical process exists to account for it. According to calculations, if they are as distant as many astronomers think they are, the total energy emitted by a quasar in one second would supply all of the Earth's electrical energy needs for a billion years.

Radio galaxies are located on the fringes of visibility. These emit radio waves millions of times more powerful than the emissions of a normal spiral galaxy. No one knows what these peculiar galaxies are.

Supernovas are large stars at their lives' ends whose final collapses generate violent explosions, blowing the surface layers out into space. There, the materials of the exploded stars mix with other material of the universe, primarily hydrogen. Later in the history of the galaxy, other stars are formed out of this mixture. The sun is one of these stars; it contains the debris of countless others that exploded before the sun was born.

So the Space Shuttle will benefit mankind in a number of ways. Not only will it reduce the cost of space flight, but it will also give us an opportunity to improve our knowledge of the Earth, its environment and the universe.

Apollo astronauts returning from the Moon described the Earth as a 'colourful island in the vast sea of blackness'. It's our Earth, the only one we have, and the Space Shuttle will serve as a platform both to advance and exploit our knowledge and to preserve and protect it and its inhabitants.

GLOSSARY

ALT – Approach and Landing Test

AOA – Abort Once Around, emergency landing procedure after one orbit

Apollo – American manned lunar landing programme

ASSESS – Airborne Science Spacelab Experiment System Simulation

ASTP – Apollo-Soyuz Test Project

Atlantis – third Shuttle Orbiter

ATO – Abort to Orbit, procedure involving emergency landing from orbit

Ballistic – an 'up and down' suborbital trajectory

Barbecue mode – continuous spacecraft roll movement

Black hole – densely packed collapsed star

Cape Canaveral – Shuttle launch site in Florida, USA

Challenger – fifth Shuttle Orbiter

Columbia – second Shuttle Orbiter, first to fly in space

Commander – leader of Shuttle mission, chief pilot

Cone-off – no covering over Orbiter main engines

Cone-on – cover on Orbiter main engines

Crawler – transporter which carries complete Shuttle configuration to launch pad at Cape Canaveral from Vertical Assembly Building

De-orbit – manoeuvre that takes Shuttle Orbiter out of orbit into re-entry

Discovery – fourth Shuttle Orbiter

Enterprise – first Shuttle Orbiter, the first to fly, during ALT

ESA – European Space Agency

EVA – extra-vehicular activity, space-walking

External Tank – liquid oxygen, liquid hydrogen storage tank for Shuttle main engines, on which the Shuttle Orbiter flies into orbit, later jettisoned

Ferret – electronic space spy

Ferry flight – movement of Shuttle Orbiter on Boeing jumbo jet to and from launch site

Fuel cells – system that provides electrical energy from liquid oxygen and liquid hydrogen and produces water as by-product

G-forces – forces of acceleration

Galileo – pioneer Jupiter orbiter probe launched by Shuttle

Gemini – second generation US manned spacecraft

Geostationary orbit – orbit in which speed of satellite exactly matches that of the Earth's rotation. Satellite appears stationary in sky

Get-away-special – available space on Shuttle for the housing of small experiment packages

GOES – Geostationary Operational Environmental Satellite, launched by Shuttle

GPS – Navigation satellite global positioning system

Hypergolic fuels – fuels that ignite spontaneously on contact

IECM – Induced Environment Contamination Monitor, experiment on Shuttle

Intelsat – US commercial communications satellite

IUS – Inertial Upper Stage for launching payloads from Shuttle

Kennedy Space Center – civilian space agency's (NASA's) portion of Cape Canaveral missile launching site

Landsat – earth resources satellite launched by Shuttle

LDEF – Long Duration Exposure Facility launched by Shuttle

Mate-Demate facility – facility in which Shuttle Orbiter is placed on or taken off jumbo jet prior to or after ferry flights

MEA – Materials Exposure Assembly flown by Shuttle

Mercury – America's first manned spacecraft

Mission Specialist – science astronaut in charge of science experiments on Shuttle missions

Mobile launcher – platform on which Shuttle is assembled for launch in Vertical Assembly Building and is transported to the launch pad by the crawler transporter and from which the Shuttle is launched

MOL – Manned Orbital Laboratory military space base project (cancelled)

NASA – civilian US Space Agency, National Aeronautics and Space Administration

Navstar – navigation satellite

Neutron star – densely packed fast spinning collapsed star

NOAA – weather and environmental satellite

OFT – Orbital Flight Test, original designation of test flights, STS 1 to 6

OMS – Orbital Manoeuvring System

Orbiter – main component of the Space Shuttle system

Orbiter landing facility – the runway

Pad 39 – Shuttle launch site at the Kennedy Space Center
Payload bay – Shuttle Orbiter cargo hold
Payload scientists – non-astronaut crew members operating science packs
PCR – Payload Change-out Room
Pilot – pilot-astronaut, second in command
Pitch – nose up and down movement or attitude of spacecraft
Press site – observation area at Kennedy Space Center for press
Pulsar – fast-spinning collapsed star emitting regular signals
Quasar – small, extremely powerful star
RTLS – Return to Launch Site, emergency procedure during launch failure
RMS – Remote Manipulator System
Radio galaxy – distant galaxy emitting powerful radio signals
RCS – Reaction Control System used to control pitch, yaw and roll
Roll – movement of Orbiter through 360° or less of its own axis
SBS – Satellite Business Systems
SSME – Space Shuttle Main Engine
SSUS – Spinning Solid Upper Stage
SRB – Solid Rocket Boosters
STS – Space Transportation System
Skylab – US's first manned space station
Spacelab – ESA space station situated in payload bay of Orbiter during some missions
Space telescope – a Space Shuttle payload
Supernova – final explosive collapse of star
Synchronous – see *Geostationary*
TPS – Thermal Protection System of Orbiter, the heatshield
TRS – Teleoperator Retrieval System
TDRSS – Tracking and Data Relay Satellite System
VAB – Vertical Assembly Building where Shuttle is assembled for launch at Kennedy Space Center
X-15 – manned rocket plane which last flew in 1960s
Zero-g – weightlessness

Photographic Acknowledgements

Boeing Aerospace Co. 72–73; NASA 10, 12, 14, 15, 18–19, 23, 24, 25, 26, 30, 34, 35, 36, 38, 39, 42, 43, 45, 46 (top), 48, 49, 50, 51, 52, 53, 54, 55, 57, 58, 62–3, 67 (below), 70, 71, 75, 78–79, 87, 88, 89 (top), 91, 94, 95, 97, 99; Rockwell International 46 (below), 61, 65, 66, 67 (top), 86, 89 (below); TRW 77.